Electronics in 2 Hours... Artificial Intelligence in 3

George J. Whalen NY9A

GET THE STORY BEHIND AMERICAN ELECTRONICS AND AI
In 2 Hours, You'll Know How Electronics Made Our Future.
In 1 More Hour, You'll Know How We Got To Artificial Intelligence.
Connections In Time And, How All These Came About:
Tubes, Transistors, Radio, TV, Cellphones, MOSFETS, Integrated Circuits, Classic and Quantum Computers. "Moore's Law?"
"Silicon Valley?"
What's Made IBM, Apple, Amazon, Google, NVIDIA (and others) Giants?
What are: "Deepseek" and "Topological Conductors?"
Should Electronics And AI Be Taught Early In American Schools? (It Is In China!)
How a century+ of electronic advances reshaped America, our world, and opened up new possibilities for the future...things that, once, we could only dream about. You'll get electronics knowledge you didn't get yesterday...but sure can use now.
After knowing what's in here, you'll be ready for more!

PREFACE

Why You Need to 'Catch-Up': Electronics became hard-to-learn in the U.S. as the 20th century ran out. From 1985 on, not just teens, but grown-ups, too, were then, quite literally robbed of most electronics learning or hobby opportunities and any chance of high-paying tech jobs disappeared. All became suddenly "closed" here in the U.S. and "electronics" (which we Americans invented), got shipped "offshore" to cheap-labor communist China. Americans were duped and blind-sided by globalists, greedy CEOs, anti-U.S. left-wing forces, high taxes, economic pressures, evil billionaires, too many wars, inflation, corrupt, paid-off politicians, closure of *Popular Electronics* magazine, *Radio Shack, Fry's* and other electronics parts stores, higher taxes on middle-class families and higher costs of daily living. Suddenly, we were much too busy trying to make ends meet and working extra hours, to give any time to self-studying electronics. We had no spare time! So, as the 20th century headed to an end, we didn't know enough about electronics to realize that America's glorious past in it was still propelling us forward, toward the brave and very new world of *Artificial Intelligence* (AI). We couldn't see that our mystifying, growing knowledge-deficit in electronics would become *a serious, national minus factor* as the century turned. Hey! Did somebody do that to us? Were we Americans slyly "dumbed-down" by evildoers, to become mere *consumers* of electronics made *somewhere else*? While China and India relentlessly trained their children in electronics from their very first days in school, our federal bureaucracy of "education bureaucrats" fumbled and destroyed American education, turning-out kids who could neither read nor do arithmetic, neither hand-write, nor even tell you who "the father of our country" was. Despite billions of dollars taken from our taxes, annually wasted, burned-through and lost by the bloated Department .of Education, they scored highest in *failure*. (How bad was it? In a study of 40 countries' educational performance, not long ago, the U.S. ranked *awful*, at No. 40. Clearly, great changes and improvement are needed.

After the 21st Century arrived, the U.S. did rid itself of the *globalism and corruption* that cost the U.S. *90,000 vanished manufacturing plants and tens of millions of jobs*, many in electronics and tech fields. The new

Trump administration endorsed reindustrializing the U.S., and ramping-up our tech sector. It "doged" federal fraud-ridden and wasteful bureaucracies, installed financial controls, saved-billions (possibly, trillions) and set new, much higher standards of performance and excellence. The Trump administration took very positive steps to attract and encourage overseas electronics and other major manufacturing and production firms to come to America and "make their products in the U.S." The benefits to them? Zero tariffs, accelerated approvals and instant building permits for new plants, help in siting, minimal delays due to regulations, and very low taxes. First up was Softbank (Japan), then, Apple (exiting China; reshoring to the U.S. and opening in India), the UAE (United Arab Emirates), Saudi Arabia, Qatar invested huge sums, and Taiwan Semiconductor Corp., NVIDIA and many others who'd been manufacturing overseas came back. Many more made major commitments of very large sums, (adding to numbers with 9 – 12 zeroes), to build new U.S. plants, manufacture and hire, here in the U.S. Many more are expected! As American businesses (e.g. autos, electronics, AI and more) fully re-industrialize and a new Golden Era of U.S. manufacturing grows. In it, learning will bring *earning* in U.S. electronics, chip and AI businesses as these develop, expand, and create more opportunities, and as AI breeds new solutions and opportunities that rely on technical know-how. The powerful generation of needs will demand that great numbers of innovators, creators, and tech workers be ready to fill millions of big-paying jobs. So, what has already happened is sure to bring greatly expanded employment opportunities. (One technical education firm has been saying that as many as *97-million* new U.S. jobs will be created. Exact timing isn't easy to pin-down just yet but those individuals who decide to ready themselves early will have their pick, as *first-movers*. Planning, plant sitings, transfers, and funding all have lots of "moving parts" and take awhile, but, the return of manufacturing businesses to the U.S. is sure and exciting. The future looks bright…and very big!

I wrote this book because no one has ever told the amazing story of American Electronics through AI, from the start, up to now. I wanted you to have it all, in one place and easy to understand. I wanted you to see how ingenious "ideas," built on earlier "connections" helped many "small" start-ups through "funny,"often "quirky" situations, to become *immense successes!* The story of Apple's start-up as a two-man, microscopic, garage business (Chapter 28) leads us to today, where Apple has now become the largest corporation in the world, measured by market capitalization! What other inventive Americans did will also open your eyes to how much we brought into the world, through inventions and discoveries in electronics. So, your 3-Hour time-investment in this book now, provides you the chance to be up-to-date on over a century-and-a- half of electronic progress, from AI, back to Edison's day. That sure sounds like a major win to me. But if you throw-in knowing how all we did in electronics got us into AI… with all the other "connections" in between, I'd say it's well worth your time! You will see what I mean, once you get into it. You have a timeline from the start, to the next great act of electronics: *AI, the next big thing*... and it will make what comes next much easier for you to master, once you know how electronics milestones and genius ideas got us here, in one, straight-line of innovation. The reward to you will be to make the techie stuff easier to learn. and it will profit you to learn now!

When you finish this book, you will know how Americans invented electronics with assists from a few geniuses of other lands (many of who came here and became Americans). Lastly, you'll also be able to name "who-did-what-and-when" and that will help you target exactly what you want to focus on as you go deeper.

Connections. So, remember that electronics was born—American at its core—using "explained" Triode vacuum tubes in 1912. Then, it was born-again, from Transistors, invented in 1947, and now it is re-invented again, as we use all the exquisitely developed hardware, microchips, techniques, science and software to move ahead in the 21st century. We've now married electronics *functionality* and real *intellect* in the latest form of electronics: Artificial Intelligence. We are pursuing new problem-solving power in Quantum Computing. Both of these rely on and partly spring from the connections to our rich, inventive, American Electronics History.

All those wonderful achievements and connections actually trace back through time to Edison's "black spot" bulb riddle in 1886, and then, one young man's amazing discoveries toiling in his folks attic lab in 1912. You will find the "connections" story line runs through many of the story selections herein. (I learned how to look for them from the magnificent works of profoundly gifted writer and thinker, James Burke.

Electronics Began in America and Came of Age in 1912 when we understood and gained control over electron flow within the Triode Vacuum Tube. How that all happened can be understood by knowing the contributions of six key figures, starting with American inventor Thomas Edison's 1883 discovery of the "Edison Effect," the public presentations by William Preece at the British Royal Society, the 1897 discovery of the electron by J.J. Thomson, the 1904 invention of the Diode Vacuum Tube by John Ambrose Fleming, its peculiar (and unintended) advancement to the triode vacuum tube in 1906, first, accidentally, by Lee DeForest, and secondly, by the painstaking, detailed studies and writings about the way the triode tube "works," by Edwin Armstrong.

His discoveries and devotion laid the groundwork for modern American electronics. It brought us radio, TV, radar and digital computers, then transistors in 1947, silicon transistors and integrated circuits by 1952, smarter computers by 1982, quantum computing by 1998, and then began, AI technology by 2015. (There are more, finer connections, but you get the picture.)

A Thought. AI and quantum computing are connected, wonderful gifts we have been given. These, together, will bring us phenomenal advances in countless, needed, future applications. Don't be misled by Hollywood's brainless horror movies that too-often make AI the "villain." Actually, AI is the best, collaborative helper ever invented! It was sought by earlier AI thinkers but it took until we had all the previous electronic components, techniques, experience, know-how and software discoveries, and the ability to apply everything we'd made in the ever-widening history of American Electronics. AI today is a wonderful partner and it will greatly aid the expansion and proliferation of human knowledge and capabilities far beyond anything we can now dream of. It is the brain within the body of electronics, and it will have a great many "children" as we learn more of its powerful, magical capabilities.

Remember this, as you go on to do great things in the 21st century.

TABLE OF CONTENTS

DEDICATION

To my always wonderful wife

Joyce Anne Whalen

Your support and enduring belief in my dreams have been my guiding light throughout this long journey. This book is a testament to your love and encouragement. May every word in it reflect the gratitude and joy I feel for having you by my side.

Always, Your George

1

The Magic of a Powerful Idea

Before we see how American Electronics and AI grew, through long centuries of powerful, magical ideas and connections, I want to tell you the story of a long-ago, powerful idea *by an inventor from 1700s Venice.* It was so brilliant that it cannot have been anything but *magic!* My aim is to show you how one great idea not only creates more great ideas by others, but how these blossom, spread seeds and lead to even more generations of other, powerful ideas that go on and on ... and to things *indistinguishable from magic!* Let's begin.

Imagine, as you read these words, that you can hear beautiful piano music playing in the background, to set the scene.

Our brilliant inventor's name was **Bartolomeo Cristofori** and he was employed by the wealthy, ruling Medicii family of 18th century Italian royalty. Part of Bartolomeo's genius was his true devotion to making refined, wonderful musical instruments. He had made many "harpsichords" (keyboard instruments that create music by *plucking* tuned strings). These were OK for small groups and pretty good at dinners, but the music was kind of "expressionless"...every note a harpsichord sounds is *exactly* like any other note! There is no way to play it "softer," or "louder." The music is always "nice," but it cannot be performed with feeling, as might have been desired by the composer. The musician had no control over its "emotion"... its volume.

But, one day, Bartolomeo got a *brilliant idea,* near the end of the 18th century. The inventor's idea was to *strike* each string with a small, padded, rebounding hammer; one for each of the 58 keys on his instrument, when its key was pressed. And he came up with an ingenious mechanism between each key and its hammer, so that the force of a hammer-hit on each string would express *how forcefully the player pushed down a key!* Suddenly, the sound volume produced by each string became controllable by the player! This now conferred a way for the music's "emotion" to be expressed by the musician! In Italian,

Cristofori called his invention *"gravicembalo col piano e forte."* In English, this translates to: "harpsichord with soft and loud."

This marvelous new instrument became known as a *"piano forte"* (in our time, it was shortened to *"a piano."*) But, the instrument became a phenomenal hit on the music scene: Mozart, Beethoven, Bach, Chopin, Lizst, and many others all embraced the newly romantic "piano forte" and created an astonishing range of piano compositions that continue to inspire, move, and delight us today.

Piano music beguiles and romances us in myriad ways, thanks first to Cristofori's genius, but then we sense the artistry of classical compositions and the brilliant styles of modern composers and artists, such as Scott Joplin, Art Tatum, Thelonious Monk and my nephew, Michael Whalen.

Bartolomeo Cristofori's story of vision, curiosity, invention and determination demonstrates characteristics great musicians, inventors, engineers and scientists all need. A great idea can set off echoes of other great ideas that continue across time. It happened with the piano forte, echoing greatly across centuries of music.

That same phenomenon happened in America's Electronics History, which has spanned our last 167+

years! This phenomenon deserves a memorable moral, and I suggest this:

Powerful Ideas and Inventions Create Lasting Change and These Inspire More Powerful Ideas, Echoing Through Time!

Nowhere is this more evident than in American Electronics, how it grew, and how it has continued to grow in America. During its long evolution, countless brilliant individuals—the majority, exceptional Americans, but also some great minds from Canada and Europe—advanced the powerful technology of electronics, creating what can only be described as "leaps of magic." This obeys the 3rd law of the great British science fiction writer, Arthur C. Clarke, which says:

"Any sufficiently advanced technology is indistinguishable from magic."

Personally, I think the brilliant ideas and physics of electronics and AI all come from a gracious and loving God, Who seems to prefer that we, His children, conceive the magical ideas and electronic inventions, based on his gifts of laws and materials, left for us to discover. And so, the inventions come from us...making wonderful toys for all His children. So, He inspires us to have wonderful ideas and to create the *electronic "things" indistinguishable from magic*.

Just as Conforti's piano set-off wave-after-wave of great music across time, electronics has enriched us, empowered us, *and now it has given us AI.* **This will bring Americans (and the world) more divine inspiration, create more ideas and great inventions, and give us lots more magic tomorrow!** The human drive to create—whether crafting a brilliant musical instrument, capable of exquisite sound and emotion, or coding an algorithm of profound complexity—has long been guided by the belief that **what can be imagined can be made real.** As we count AI's possibilities, do recognize the "connections" in how the long history of American Electronics got us here. It's given us real power to create magic!

2

(1844–1912) The Electric Start: Before "Electronics" Came. How Ideas & Experiments Launched Telegraphy, Telephone & Radio

This time-period in America was defined by sequential innovations in electrical communication, each expanding upon the last—but all remaining passive, in nature. It was the age of signals, where devices could transmit information, but lacked amplification or control beyond simple switching mechanisms. (See Appendix 2).

The Telegraph (1844)

Samuel Morse's telegraph demonstrated electrical signaling, but real genius behind its widespread use came from Alfred Vail, who developed the Morse Code—a practical, systematic way to efficiently transmit messages. Letters and numbers were represented by "long" and "short" key-presses. In print, these were represented by combinations of "dashes" and "dots." A dash sent a long click to a sounder at the receive point. A dot was a shorter sound. The receiving operator had to be skilled at hearing the combinations that formed the different letters and would handwrite the message. The first public telegraph message, "What hath God wrought," was sent on May 24, 1844, marking the dawn of long-distance electrical communication.

The Telephone (1876)

Alexander Graham Bell's patent for the telephone issued on March 7, 1876 and introduced real-time voice transmission through electrical signals, making communication vastly more personal and immediate. The telephone improved upon the telegraph by transmitting continuous speech waveforms instead of discrete electrical pulses. Early telephones used carbon microphones that varied in electrical resistance as a diaphragm was moved by a person's speaking. The varying electrical current sent over the line caused a small electromagnet to vibrate at the speech-rate, converting the current changes into vibrations of a metal diaphragm, thus creating speech-sound.

Wireless Experiments (1860s–1890s)

Mahlon Loomis, in the 1860s, had experimented with wireless telegraphy, hinting at radio's potential. Too many have unjustly limited his accomplishment by citing his dentistry day-job. But, Loomis actually came from a high-level science-rich family and was way-ahead in his time. It was not until 1886 that Heinrich Hertz demonstrated the existence of electromagnetic (radio) waves using electric spark-gap devices. Loomis' 600-ft.-long copper wire antennas were suspended from kites. A ground was used. Current was provided through a switch, from atmospheric electricity. When closed and opened, it resulted in a "square-wave" current pulse to the transmit antenna-ground, which was likely self-resonant at some low, radio frequency. This generated an impulse electromagnetic (EM) wave, from the infinite harmonics in the square-wave. This EM wave was radiated, and intercepted by the 18-mile-away identical kite-antenna at the receiving location, self-resonant at the same frequency as the transmit kite antenna. The arrival of the low-frequency impulse EM caused deflection of the receiving galvanometer between the antenna and ground. Remember, it was an experiment, done by Loomis in 1868 and not yet a practical device for signaling. But it was radio.

Marconi's Spark Wireless Telegraph (1896)

Guglielmo Marconi was fascinated by radio, quite rich, and able to afford the best electrical consultants, like John Ambrose Fleming. These geniuses borrowed and progressed Heinrich Hertz's spark EM wave lab discovery into a practical, salable, radio-telegraphy communication system. By 1896, Marconi successfully transmitted some spark wireless signals, increasing distance to transatlantic radio-telegraphy by 1901, with a new detector. The fault in earlier work had been the receiving device (a Branly Coherer). This very crude and insensitive device could only detect the strongest, high-powered, spark radio signals. The *diode vacuum tube*, a much more-sensitive detection device, was invented by John Ambrose Fleming. (See Chapter 4.) It paved the way for future success of radio technology, but signals, then, were still only radio-*telegraphy*, sent by high-voltage spark transmitters. In 1912, the sinking *Titanic* had a Marconi-manufactured spark wireless, and two Marconi-trained operators. The rescue ship, *Carpathia,* had a Marconi wireless and one Marconi operator. (This early combination of men-and-machines actually saved 708 people who would have died otherwise, after *Titanic* sank, in April, 1912.)

Reginald Fessenden Takes Radio from "Spark" To "Speech" – Before Vacuum Tubes! (1906)

We owe high praise and honor to Reginald Fessenden, who taught radio to speak! Though the brilliant son of a Canadian-born mother, he claimed U.S. citizenship through his American-born father. He was the true inventor of AM Radio voice transmission (amplitude modulation) and actually pioneered radio broadcasting in 1906.

Fessenden had taught college-level mathematics and engineering at Purdue and later in Pittsburgh. But he yearned to do electrical engineering work, so he moved to New York, worked for Thomas Edison (at Edison General Electric, which would later become GE) and then for George Westinghouse.

Next, Fessenden began working on spark wireless equipment and devised spark transmitters and receiving apparatus for radiotelegraphy stations. But, his real goal was voice transmission. Neither the raspy spark transmitters, nor the insensitive coherer detectors of the time could handle complex waveforms like human voice sounds. The sound from them was simply awful.

To improve the situation, he devised the electrolytic detector, which used a cats-whisker wire, dipped into a liquid, to make a better radio detector. Its sensitivity was far greater than a coherer. He patented it and it was adopted by the U.S. Navy. (It is said that Lee DeForest tried to copy and claim Fessenden's detector, but he was rebuffed by a patent infringement lawsuit. This was a behavior DeForest would become known for.

But Fessenden pressed-on. Seeking further improvements in voice transmission equipment, on a cold December 23 of 1900, Fessenden and his assistant, Alfred Thiessen, set up equipment in two shacks with 50-foot antenna towers, one mile apart, on Cobb Island, Maryland. Thiessen went to one shack with his electrolytic detector and radio receiving equipment, while Fessenden and his voice-transmitting radio equipment (an alternator) went to the other. There was a landline telegraph link between the two shacks. After several tries with very poor receiving results, the steam-engine powering Fessenden's alternator transmitter suddenly began to run faster and more smoothly than earlier. He grabbed the mike and said, "One, two, three, four. Is it snowing where you are, Mr. Thiessen? If it is, telegraph back and let me know." Thiessen heard him much more clearly. It was the first voice message ever transmitted by radio.

Emboldened by this success, Fessenden set up the National Electric Signaling Company. He built an antenna tower at Brant Rock (near Boston in Massachusetts and erected another tower on the coast of Scotland. In January 1906, Fessenden tested his new creation by sending a two-way radio-telegraph message across the Atlantic Ocean. Fessenden had created workable equipment and stations of his own design with full-message capability. Now, his aim was to transmit *two-way voice messages* across the Atlantic and make Marconi's spark radio-telegraphy obsolete! This stunning plan brought more development work that continued over a period of six years, culminating in his actually transmitting the very first amplitude-modulated (AM) radio "broadcast" on Christmas Eve 1906, from his Brant Rock. MA home.

The program's content was homemade and via a carbon microphone. Fessenden spoke, did a Bible reading and played the violin, and his family sang Christmas carols. This program was actually heard by radio operators aboard a number of U.S. Navy ships and United Fruit ships in the Atlantic, off the east coast. All were amazed to hear voices and music in place of the usual hiss of sparks!

This incredible event marked the origin of all AM voice radiotelephone technology—as well as the beginning of broadcasting. What makes this even more remarkable was that it took place in what was still the Electric Start Era, still dominated by early spark transmitters. It was Fessenden's genius that upgraded his radio technology and led him to use a high-frequency (88 kHz) produced by a unique AC generator called an *alternator.* You see, Fessenden brilliantly knew that to maximize the sound clarity and fidelity of his radio signal, he needed to have as *pure* a radio-frequency carrier wave as he could get. It had to be as close to a *sine wave* as possible. No spark transmitter device could do that! His brilliant answer was *a special, high-frequency alternator*. It needed to be a super-fast, rotary mechanical generator, very difficult to make and quite dangerous. (They were known to fly apart from their very high speeds and rotational stresses.) But, these unique machines could theoretically produce near-sinewave-smooth radio-frequency energy at 50–100 kiloHertz... exactly what Fessenden needed!

Years earlier, Fessenden had done engineering work at the original Edison General Electric Company. He still had many talented engineering friends and associates there, and they now had much added freedom to work on projects, since Edison was gone. He had been "retired" by financier J. P. Morgan (that's how The Edison General Electric Company became *General Electric: GE*).

So, beginning in 1904, Fessenden called on his old-friends at GE, to build him a *high-frequency alternator* (a big, motor-driven AC generator with an electrical output frequency way up in the radio-frequency range of *60–90 kilohertz*. It took awhile, but his friends came through. The alternator was designed and built by a team led by Ernst Alexandreson and shipped to Fessenden, who completed setting it up at his Brant Rock, MA home in August of 1906. He had arranged to "amplitude modulate" the alternator's radio-frequency output, using a carbon microphone for sound input. Fessenden connected the resistive microphone in series with the battery supply, so that the current controlling the alternator's output amplitude was varied in proportion to voice or other sound striking the mike diaphragm. This created the 88 kHz AM signal.

On Christmas Eve 1906, he, his wife and children went "on the air," broadcasting the AM radio signal of his violin, a bible reading, and his family's carol singing. This AM signal was radiated from his 402 foot radio antenna. The signal was received by the U.S. Navy and United Fruit Company ships, up and down the waters offshore the entire eastern U.S. It was the first AM voice and music radio broadcast ever made.

But, despite the results and brilliance of Fessenden's invention, Marconi's powerfully influential connections in industry, government and royal quarters ruthlessly blocked his business efforts at every turn! He was denied permissions by the British and Canadian governments to set up commercial stations, because these governments had vested interests in Marconi's established operations. Radio, had "learned to speak" in 1906! But it would take longer for *AM Radio Broadcasting* to come.

How Electronics Got Underway (1912). Remember, in 1906, we were still in the "Electric Start" phase, which preceded "electronics"...there simply weren't any "tubes"... yet. The peculiar discovery path of actual, vacuum tube triode tubes...and the discovery by Edwin Armstrong of their technical characteristics, gave mankind the very-first active, electronic device. But, then, other techies had to learn, create circuits and invent... manufacturers had to design and provide tubes and parts... and everyone had to get to work! It was found that tubes could be used to make radio signals and to modulate and control the current flows of electrons within circuits.

3

How Vacuum Tube Electronics Finally Came, Through The Amazing Ideas & Connections By 6 Men. (1880–1912)

IT TOOK 32 long years to happen... for each of these men to have a hand in getting ELECTRONICS going. I found the clues and connections between them and I present the magical story here.

(1880) Thomas A. Edison & His Black-Spot Lightbulbs

It all began with his Light Bulbs. Customers complained that the glass bulbs developed odd "Black Spots," inside the glass, over time. Edison's incandescent light bulbs had a conductive filament, electrically heated until it glowed, enclosed in a clear, glass bulb, emptied to a vacuum. An electric current was supplied to the filament by wires in the glass, which connected to a threaded metal support that could be screwed-into an electrical power socket.

Now, this might have described almost any early light bulbs ever fabricated. But, I believe that the ones invented by Thomas Edison, about 1879, and patented in 1880, led directly to discovering *the technology of vacuum tubes*.

You remember vacuum tubes, right? They reigned over 20th century technology and made radio and electronics into household words.

Many inventors, like Joseph Swan, Marcellin Jobard, Frederick de Moleyns, and others all the way back to 1761, had caused materials to glow by passing electricity through filaments in bulbs. But none of those inventors had Edison's drive and curiosity! He wanted to make incandescent lighting into a successful, big business; one supported by a vast electrical distribution system of DC generators and wiring. It was to be "all-in-one," as a concept. It was his huge curiosity and drive that powered Edison's intense desire to study and know every detail of his invention.

People had two honest complaints about Edison's incandescent lamps: they "burnt-out" too soon; and, their clear glass bulbs would get "black spots," in use. Edison went to work to discover "why?"

Edison did not know this back then, but the culprit causing his blackened bulbs is now known as *"thermionic emission"* and it is really quite simple. When you heat a filament, you boil lots of electrons off it. A cloud of these tiny electrons goes into the vacuum in the bulb. These settle onto the glass, in coats. Ultimately, those electrons form a black spot. The filament also becomes brittle as the lamp is used. Each time the lamp is turned on, the filament is physically stressed. Eventually it breaks

If the lamp is being fed by DC (as it was back then) the black spot inside the bulb would always show by the end connected to the positive side of the power line (since electrons have a negative charge, they are attracted there). Of course, this was all completely unknown, until the electron was discovered in 1897, by scientist J. J. Thomson.

But Edison wanted to stop the blackening *now*. So, he experimented with a large number of possible cures. He wrapped wires and shaped metal pieces around the bulb; he put foils and plates inside the bulb, with connections through the glass for electrical tests; he had test sample bulbs of each experiment made, with more wires, metal foils and plates sealed inside. Only one result came about: by themselves, the added parts did nothing to stop the blackening!

Edison was furious!

Then, in 1883, Edison tried an electrical hookup. He connected an internal metal plate he'd put inside a bulb sample to a 22.5-volt battery's positive terminal, and connected its negative terminal to the filament. Then, he put a galvanometer (a current-measuring instrument) into the battery's positive line connected to the metal plate.

And, the meter showed a current flow!

Huh? Now, that really had Edison perplexed! He reasoned that there was no direct connection between the filament and plate. But, the galvanometer clearly showed an electric current flow between the filament and the plate! Why?

This was a mystery to Edison! Since electrons wouldn't be discovered by J. J. Thomson until 1897, Edison could be forgiven for not knowing "why?" But, his curiosity and drive to know everything led him to apply for a patent. So, he obtained U.S. Patent 307,301, issued in 1883. Edison had no clear idea how he'd use it. Maybe as a voltage-measuring device?

(1886) The Second Man: William H. Preece, Head Of The British Royal Society

William H. Preece was a well-known English scientist and also head of the British Royal Society. Edison had written to him about his "black spots and odd current measurement" and (about 1886) Preece came over to the U.S. to pay Edison a visit. The two men got along quite well (no doubt over brandy and cigars after excellent meals) and Edison was delighted to share his experiences about his inquiry into why his light bulbs turned black and how a galvanometer showed a current flow between unconnected parts, when he thought it shouldn't have. He repeated the experiments for Preece and copious notes were taken.

After seeing these phenomena for himself, Preece was astounded, but he could offer no explanation. Yet, he was eager to share them with his colleagues and audiences at the Royal Society of England, back in London. So, Edison had many lamp samples made up for him with all the foils, wires and plates inside, and Preece took these back with him to England, along with his notes about Edison's experiments. He later wrote and presented papers on what he called: "the Edison Effect" and gave Royal Society public demonstrations to packed audiences.

(1897) Scientist J. J. Thomson, and Consulting Engineer John Ambrose Fleming

In 1897, scientist J. J. Thomson published his HUGE discovery of the electron! That same year, John Ambrose Fleming, a British consulting electrical engineer in late 19th century England, was then the top "go-to-guy" for anyone in need of electrical solutions. He had a prestigious client list. Among them Guglielmo Marconi (See Appendix 2).

Fleming was also a highly respected Fellow of the British Royal Society. He attended the meetings, saw Preece's demonstrations and read his papers on the Edison Effect. Fleming thought long and hard about what was happening inside Edison's black-spotted light bulbs. But, he now knew something more from his scientific reading of Thomson's discovery! The spots were clearly from electrons! Fleming had put two-and-two together and concluded that the mysterious "Edison Effect" current flow Preece had seen on the galvanometer was actually electron current streaming through Edison's bulb, from the hot filament to the positive plate! He knew he was right when he saw the current flow stop when the plate polarity was made negative. (Electrons, being negative, are repelled by a negative charge.) This gave Fleming the idea to invent *the diode* vacuum tube: the first two-element tube... and that became the "opening act" of electronics!

Fleming's diode vacuum tube invention could rectify (change AC into DC, because current could only flow to the plate during the positive half-cycle; it stopped on each negative half-cycle) and so the diode tube could also be used to detect radio signals with far better sensitivity: something his client (Mr. Marconi) urgently needed to replace the dreadfully insensitive "coherer" detectors that had been used in his earlier, lukewarm Trans-Atlantic radio-telegraphy experiments! Fleming's U.S. Patent issued on his diode vacuum tube in 1904.

(1906) PhD & Con-Man: Lee DeForest

Lee DeForest had a PhD from Yale. He was also a person who had a large, ongoing need for income. He had been married four times and divorced three. (Big alimony.) He also had been involved in some very sketchy stock swindles that narrowly left him just out-of-jail, but quite deep in legal debt. So, he always needed income.

One of his specialties was finding new patents he could "modify" slightly. Then, he would apply for a new "improvement" patent (and possibly, get it). Doing this, his sketchy patent could ride on the original patent's fame and earn some royalties to help pay-off his many legal bills (and ex-wives). He had used this scheme against many well-known, legitimate inventors. A number of lawsuits for patent infringement had been brought against DeForest, but some weren't, so he occasionally got lucky... and his lawyers (and ex-wives) got paid. But, his legal expenses kept on climbing!

When Fleming's U.S. patent on the diode vacuum tube issued, DeForest had slyly gone to work, making his own dodgy patent application. He drew-up tubes with all manner of plate shapes and foils inside, as well as a filament. In one, he placed a "grid shaped" screen, between the filament and plate. But the patent application text made no mention of the "grid." It only spoke of the device being used as a "detector." There was no mention of "amplification" being possible by use of it. DeForest's patent was silent on that, and there was no mention of "how his tube worked or what it could do." All DeForest wanted from his "detector" patent was some dollars of income. He could not explain it and his "invention" was only a ruse. He called his peculiar tube "an Audion," saying he believed its operation "came from ions of gas within the tube." (This, of course, was later proven untrue.) His fanciful explanations brought him ridicule as an inventor.) But, his detector patent issued and showed a grid, even if it was not explained. So the

Triode Vacuum Tube had been "kind-of-invented," even if no one, including DeForest, knew how it worked!

(1912) Edwin H. Armstrong:
The Father of Electronics!

He discovered and explained how the Triode works in 1912. Though Lee De Forest had "sort-of" patented the triode in 1906, that patent lacked a disclosure; it was silent about "the function of the grid." So, the tube was not at all understood, until Armstrong demonstrated its ability to amplify, generate signals and switch, the very same year that the *Titanic* sank. Young Armstrong had just graduated as an electrical engineer from Columbia University. He was first in his class and his professors loved him for his genius. They gave him a graduation gift of two costly, Deforest Audion triode vacuum tubes. But, their gift to their top electrical engineering student had come with an extremely tough assignment: to study and experiment with those DeForest triode tubes, in great detail; then, write and publish technical papers about how the tubes worked, and how they could be used.

DeForest's U.S. patent only called his tube "a detector" (like Fleming's) and offered nothing else. Throughout his life, DeForest could not satisfactorily explain how his tube worked. But, Armstrong, working alone in the attic lab he'd made in his parent's home on Warburton Avenue in Yonkers, NY, devoted himself to measuring, experimenting and unraveling the puzzle of DeForest's Audion, in exceptional detail. He discovered the true operating characteristics of the triode vacuum tube for the very first time; then, he wrote and published the details... *and so, the era of U.S. electronics actually began in 1912* and everyone learned from what Armstrong discovered. His research rigorously explained exactly how DeForest's Audion Triode Tube operated. For months, he had assiduously studied the triode and revealed its secrets. He explained how and why it amplified. He discovered regeneration, and audio and radio-frequency oscillation. (Years Later, he went on to devise the superheterodyne radio receiver, which became the American standard radio design; and much later, he invented and pioneered the entire process of wideband FM broadcasting!) Through Edwin Amstrong's great genius, electronics was truly born as the American technology that would rule the twentieth century and inspire a new era of engineering development to enrich the knowledge of all mankind.

How American Electronics came to be is the tale that will be told by the next chapters, describing the many electronic inventions by other Americans. And in that spirit, the magic of our stroll through America's Electronic History continues.

When Armstrong had discovered all of the triode tube's secrets, his solid, engineering data articles (In *Electrical World* magazine and presentations and proceedings with the Institute of Radio Engineers) opened the way for other techies everywhere to know how to make use of the the vacuum tube triode. Electronics grew. New inventions soared. The triode was revolutionary; it was an *active element*—it didn't merely transmit or switch signals; it could also strengthen, modify or amplify them. So, these marked the true beginning of electronics:

Amplification: Signals could be boosted, allowing for weaker transmissions to be heard more clearly.

Oscillation & Modulation: The triode enabled precisely tuned, continuous-wave radio, capable of replacing spark-gap transmitters and making broadcasting possible.

Electronic Control: For the first time, electrical signals could actively manipulate other circuits, and that led directly to modern computing.

So, while The Electric Start phase laid the groundwork, it was the triode tube that transformed this interest into electronics—giving rise to radio, television, radar, computers, transistors, television, cellular phones, super-computers, integrated circuits, quantum computers, and now, artificial intelligence.

4

How Triode Vacuum Tubes And Transistors Work

LET'S TAKE A break and look at the operation of the active devices that make electronics possible. The triode vacuum tube and the transistor both are true "active devices." Both can control a large current flow through an output circuit, in proportion to a small voltage applied to the input circuit. I hope this will be the very best, easiest description you've ever read about how the major active devices of electronics...the vacuum electron tube and the transistor...work. I am not going to bore you with pointless details, as older (and largely outmoded) transistor theory did. Instead, I'll just cover triode tubes and MOSFETS, so that you can how each of these devices can control electron flow in a circuit. When you grasp those basics, you can concentrate on other details that make electronics so darn interesting! Just learn how these active devices work, first!

How A Triode Vacuum Tube Works. We'll start with the three-element triode vacuum tube. This has a cathode (source of electrons), a grid (input and control element), and an anode (or plate, the output element). These are concentric and usually sealed inside an evacuated glass bulb. The vacuum allows the free passage of tiny electrons. (If air molecules were present, they'd block the electrons.) Each of the tube's elements is connected to an external pin that is sealed to the glass bulb. The pins allow the tube to be inserted into a socket, for easy changeover. (Tubes have a finite life, like light bulbs, and need to be changed as performance declines.)

The cathode is the common negative element of the input and output, and it is a resistive (heater) device, when energized by an electrical current source, it gives-off a continuous cloud of electrons. These negatively charged tiny particles go nowhere if the nearby grid has no charge. But, if we apply a low, alternating signal input voltage between the grid and cathode (that is, it goes up (+), then, down (-), the grid will attract and pass more electrons when the input signal swings positive, and repel electrons when the signal goes negative. This causes the signal-voltage-varying current-flow of electrons passing through the grid, to enter into the area of influence near the positively DC-charged plate. the varying current flow attracted to the plate's high DC voltage charge will cause the output signal to go up and down, creating a larger version of the input signal voltage applied between the grid and cathode. So, the output (between plate and cathode) will be a larger plate current, but varying exactly the way the signal voltage swings up and down on the grid. This is called *amplification*.

If I choose to make the tube act as a switch, I can apply a sufficiently negative DC voltage between the grid and cathode, in place of a varying signal, that will instantly stop the flow of electrons, thus switching-off the plate current. If I remove the negative DC input, plate current flow will immediately resume, making the triode a fastacting switch.

There you have the basic operation of a triode vacuum tube. There are other great configurations for specific applications, but if you get this one clear in your mind you'll know most of what you need to know about how any kind of vacuum tube operates. The rest can come later, from other sources, if you choose to go on.

How A MOSFET Transistor Works. We now leave vacuum tubes behind and enter the world of solid-state devices. All transistors have unlimited life, but MOSFETs are rather like tubes in some ways, and can do the same kinds of jobs as tubes. But, their mechanism of action is a bit different. Earlier varieties of semiconductor materials were used to make transistors, starting with germanium. Eventually, though, silicon won out. Using a planar process invented by Jean Hoerni in 1959 at Fairchild Semiconductor, the mass-production of silicon transistors protected by a layer of silicon dioxide became possible. So, metal oxide semiconductor field effect transistors (MOSFETs) became the most widely used transistor type and soon brought integrated circuit technology (like the electronics in your cellphone). In digital circuits, these devices consume little or no current except when switching states and have fast switching speeds.

Because MOSFETs have become the most widely manufactured transistor device in the history of electronics (as of now, about 16 *sextillion* have been manufactured), there seems no reason to even mention other transistor types, (which you may never even see).

Inside the MOSFET is a "silicon sandwich." There is a Gate element centered on top of a Body, but insulated from it. The left third of the Body is the Source (where electrons enter), while the right third of the Body is the Drain (where electrons exit). The middle section of the Body is influenced by the "field" at the Gate (which controls the flow of electrons between the Source and Drain, in step with an applied electrical signal.) These three make up a *field-effect transistor*. Three wires: Gate, Source and Drain lead out to connect with the circuitry. When a positive signal is applied between the Gate and Source, the electrostatic field it exerts creates a conducting charge on the Body area below it, so that a proportional electron current flows between the Source and the Drain. Thus, the Drain current rises and falls with the Gate signal, creating an amplified output. When the signal falls to zero, there is no current drawn from the power supply. As in the tube, if I use a DC voltage between Gate and Source, I have a switch, The on-off switching of MOSFETs is very fast making it today's prime active element choice of digital device designers.

5

How Transistors, ICs And Other Magic Came About

For a few minutes, let's jump ahead to 1947. That's when three genius physicists at New York's Bell Labs found the same sort of "tube-like functions" in American-invented *transistors.* These solid-state devices could amplify and switch, like tubes, but they worked very differently, were long-lived and quite useful, lots cooler and more-compact. Years later, we advanced to *silicon transistors*, and then, to integrated circuits (ICs), with lots of mini transistors, parts and micro-printed wiring, allowing us to make smaller, smarter digital computers. That led us to smarter software, easier, natural language programming, Silicon Valley, Moore's Law, and then, to large-scale integration (lots and lots of super-tiny transistors, circuitry and interconnections, all on one silicon chip); then, to Machine Learning,

Neural Networks, Artificial Intelligence (AI) and use of Large Language Models (LLMs) for AI training. So, as you can see, one great development led to another and America's Electronic History grew as American geniuses added to the magic we already had!

Now, we have passed through the AI front door. We're inside, and heading down the hall, toward smarter and smarter artificial intelligence, hopefully on the way to artificial general intelligence (AGI). We have the thoughts and insights of Alan Turing, John von Neumann, plus other American AI leaders to guide us, and a wellendowed and exploding electronics manufacturing and U.S. AI industry, producing in a new Golden Era. And, of course, we will be using the strengths of all the electronics we've discovered over 167+ years. It's a great time to be in electronics! (Magic!)

6

How Triode Vacuum Tubes Began Electronics In 1912

LET'S GET BACK to the beginning, in 1912. Then, we'll come forward in time (one chapter at a time) and see how electronics progressed.

We have a lot of brilliance to celebrate! It's because we now have added the amazing dimension of intelligence, to functionality in our active, electronic devices. I'll start with some, here. Then, in each chapter we'll unwind the story of a great accomplishment in American Electronics History that is important to us today. You will know a lot as we move through the years and finally arrive at "Now," where electronics blossoms into quantum computing and Artificial Intelligence. Right now, the first generation of Americans exist who will live surrounded by machines, devices, instruments, conveniences and services that are non-human, yet embody human-like intellect, access to vast amounts of data and huge reservoirs of knowledge and answers, all immediately accessible. At no other time in all of humankind's history has anything like such wealth, due to American Electronics ever been possible. Think about it... until the astounding impact comes to you that you are fortunate to be here, in this truly amazing time.

Back in 1912, hundreds of American techies quickly learned from Armstrong's articles. Triode tubes and how they worked, then gave engineers and inventors the magic, new, capabilities of electronic amplification, switching, and radio-frequency energy generation. All those functions were used to create new circuitry for radio, then, broadcasting, then, television, long-distance telephony, and later, digital computers (first, with tubes, in the classic "0-and-1" binary style; then, in radar, cellular phones, and later, FM broadcasting, (also by Armstrong) then, the encore of many conveniences, but using solid-state devices. Next came, *silicon transistors and ICs.* These ushered-in powerful, personal computers, then, super-computers, then, quantum-type computers, artificial intelligence, smart machines (robots), satellites and networks.

So, as you can see, Armstrong got this party started,

but his powerful ideas set off echoes of invention, by many others, across time. He truly *deserves the title: Father of Electronics,* and the admiration and respect of all).

Uses For Triode Tubes. The early growth of American Electronics after WW I (1918) was rapid. By the 1920s, commercial U.S. radio broadcasting and communications were starting, though their advance was slowed by The U.S. Great Depression of the '30s. Still, electronic amplifiers with triode tubes were being used in long-distance telephones, movies and the music recording industry. Also, AM radio broadcasting came and the public took BIG notice. Radio became "king" in America of the 1930s. And, when World War II came, electronics was put into uniform and wartime service. At home, radio kept America posted.

Germanium Transistor Invention: In 1945, WW II ended and soon after, the first germanium transistor was invented (1947) at New York's Bell Labs, by Drs. John Bardeen, Walter Brattain and William Shockley. But, vacuum tubes ruled: in ENIAC, the first electronic digital computer, in microwaves, high power radio transmission, and television, until the mid-1980s, but solid-state devices (transistors) took over in all other electronics. In April 1955, the Model 608 digital computer was the first IBM U.S. product to use all-transistor circuits; with more than 3,000 germanium transistors. This led IBM's then-president, Thomas J. Watson Jr. to rule that all future IBM products would use transistors as the active design devices. Thereafter, transistors became exclusively used by industry, for digital computer logic and peripherals.

MOSFET Silicon Transistors Arrive: Because early transistors were big and bulky, the MOSFET (Metal-Oxide Semiconductor Field-Effect Transistor) was invented by Dr. Mohammed Attalla and Dawon Kahng at Bell Labs. It was the first, truly rugged, silicon, compact-form transistor that could be greatly miniaturized and mass-produced for a very wide range of uses. (Silicon comes from sand; and it's rugged, and far more sturdy than germanium. It's a cheap and plentiful semiconductor. It revolutionized the electronics industry, made large-scale integrated circuits possible, and it has become the world's most widely used electronic component. Older, germanium transistors, now infrequently used, are current-driven devices and operate very differently from MOSFETs (though their functions remain somewhat similar). You can forget then for now and avoid confusion; learn about them later, or maybe, not at all.

Integrated Circuits: In late 1956, William Shockley left Bell Labs in New York and moved west, to Mountain View, California, to care for his ailing mother. Wanting to keep busy in his semiconductor development work, he started Shockley Semiconductor Laboratory, in Santa Clara County. He hired 8 brilliant people to help him develop silicon semiconductors. But, there are lots of 'quirks' in silicon's surface conductivity and characteristics, and these "bad guys" frequently stymied progress. Experiments failed often and tempers flared daily. Ongoing frustrations led to unpleasant, frequent disagreements between Shockley and all of his top, scientist staffers. The atmosphere of the laboratory became very toxic. Shockley's entire staff of eight was on the point of quitting. (He was brilliant, but unbearable.)

Back at Bell Labs, NY on the east coast, Dr. Mohammed Atalla was also working with silicon, experiencing the same kinds of failures that bedeviled Shockley and his staff, Atalla came up with a brilliant "assist:" a surface oxide "passivation process" that stopped silicon from reacting badly. Experiments now became successful and silicon transistors became cheap and plentiful! Atalla and his partner, Dawon Kahng went on to invent silicon field-effect transistors, an entirely different family of transistor devices from the original germanium point-contact and junction transistors. They named them: *metal oxide semiconductor fieldeffect transistors*, or MOSFETs, for short.

Inexplicably, Bell Labs on the east coast chose to fund other work and overlooked the MOSFET, so it languished on the shelf, wasting much time. Shockley tried to get Bell Labs staffers to move west, to his lab, but they stayed put! (Perhaps word of his mercurial temper had gotten around.)

How "Silicon Valley" Developed: What happened next was incredible! Sherman Fairchild (of east coast Fairchild Camera and instrument in Syosset, NY) had attended a conference in 1957, where he'd heard Robert Noyce make a passionate, visionary presentation about his concept of a silicon-based integrated circuit (IC) and his belief in its powerful future! Noyce brought seven other colleagues with him – all had resigned at once from Shockley's super-toxic, very frictional employment. So, Sherman Fairchild created Fairchild Semiconductor, hired all eight, and installed Jack S. Kilby and Robert Noyce as its leaders. Gordon Moore (another of the eight) later teamed up with Noyce in 1968 to form Intel Corporation. This was the beginning of "Silicon Valley." (A newspaper coined that name... and it stuck.) Jack S. Kilby received the Nobel Prize in 2000 for his integrated circuit contribution.

IC Computer Memory Products Nourished Intel: The silicon process innovation was aided by another developed by Jean Hoerni. Combined, it was like opening the floodgates for the modern, silicon electronics era. The planar process allowed for the mass production of integrated circuits, which are the very heart and soul of today's AI, gadgets, and computers. (It's fascinating how the contributions from over half a century ago are still humming inside our smartphones and computers.) These breakthroughs directly led to the Electronics we just can't live without today. (That now includes A.I.)

Moore's Law: It's NOT physics. It's economics! The more transistors you can squeeze onto an IC, the *more data* it can hold. By shrinking down the size of MOSFETs to mini-micro-or-*nano*meter-size, more and more transistors can fit on each, new IC silicon chip.

In studying this, Gordon Moore (co-founder of Intel) made the canny discovery (in 1965) that the number of transistors on a microchip *doubles* approximately every two years, while the *cost* of computers is reduced. This has driven exponential growth in computing power, and that has profoundly impacted the electronics industry, leading to smaller, more powerful, and more affordable electronic devices over time, and opening the door to AI. While it has held true for several decades, it is becoming increasingly difficult to maintain due to physical and technical limitations in semiconductor manufacturing. Nonetheless, Moore's Law continues to be a useful, guiding principle for innovation in the technology sector.

Integrated Circuits: As the complexity of digital circuitry grew, physical size problems arose. For example, the performance of a computer circuit depends most on its speed. If its components are too large, the wires interconnecting them need to be long. So, signals take more time to go through the circuit, slowing-down the computer. The invention of integrated circuitry on silicon chips solved this problem, making it possible to form all components and tiny interconnecting "wiring" on the same chip. So, integrated circuits could be made much smaller, and manufacturing could be automated. In 2008, large MOSFET processor ICs became commercially available. Now it's possible to have a cell phone with as many as a billion tiny transistors in its IC. (Fascinating, isn't it? It's amazing how far electronic technology has come and where it might go next!) How electronics and AI progressed to the end of the 20th century is covered in all the later chapters of this book. Here's a brief synopsis.

Broadcast Radio. After Mahlon Loomis' 1868 Mountain-top radio experiment, wireless had had a long, unhappy, impoverished childhood as it suffered under the painful shadow of the U.S. Civil War and Recovery. It took until the early years of the 20th century for radio to actually take root in the U.S. But, the first World War intervened. Then, In the 1920s U.S. radio broadcasting came and brought the thrill of listening to people everywhere in the U.S. It grew and kept people glued to their AM radio receivers. The idea of receiving news, messages and music magically from far away, by invisible radio waves, was very appealing. Everyone got hooked... we listened in our cars, too. But listening wasn't enough. We wanted to talk.

So, AT&T Radio-Telephones Came. But, they were big, analog, channel-limited, and always busy. To partly solve this, analog cellular car phones came about. Then, many years later, a genius black engineer at Bell Labs, **Jesse E. Russell, changed cellular technology over to digital** (**1980-88**)**...** and, suddenly, cell phones were out of the car trunk and could be made small enough to be put into our pockets and purses, to make us "mobile. This advance was profound! It is rivaled by only a few earlier achievements. Russell deserved a medal, a parade and a party thrown by the entire world!

Back In the 19th century, it had been a Scot who changed the world, the great mathematical and physics genius, James Clerk Maxwell, who developed and published his Theory of Electromagnetism in 1873. This mathematical insight enabled us to later understand and explain radio. His twenty equations predicted that light, magnetism and electrical waves all were to be found within the Electromagnetic Spectrum and he explained that the magnetics laws found by Gauss and Faraday worked just exactly like the electrical laws of Ampere. And so, he proved that light, magnetism and electricity all come from the same electromagnetic force, and that the movement of electrons everywhere is at the very heart of this force!

> ***To put it more simply, electricity is produced when electrons "flow" (as a current) from one physical location to another. And, magnetism is produced when electrons "spin" in the same direction. And, light is produced when electrons "shift" from a higher to a lower energy state... and, in doing that, each electron releases a photon. Now you know it all!***

The only problem with Maxwell's equations was that you needed to be a super-math-genius to understand them! For Maxwell, this was easy. He had been a professor of physics at Kings College, London in his teens... and its dean at age 25! By 1873, Maxwell completed his Treatise on Electricity and Magnetism with great impact on the scientific community. But, the difficult math of his theory was kinda slow to spread, because it was hard to understand.

It was Oliver Heaviside (the self-taught, English physicist, telegrapher, and genius-son of a London blacksmith) who brilliantly reduced Maxwell's 20 mind-bending equations to just *four*, and who created a new form of mathematics, called *vector calculus*, to solve them! (So though we still call them "Maxwell's Equations," now you know the rest of the story!)

Ultimately, Maxwell's treatise became as renowned as Sir Isaac Newton's *Principia Mathematica*, the great physics book which gave us calculus and revolutionized physics for the first time, several centuries earlier. But, it was Maxwell's published Treatise on Electromagnetism that laid the foundation for all electrical and electronic engineering in our 20th century! Now, let's get on with our American Electronics timeline.

7

(1922–1935) AM Radio Broadcasting Creates a U.S. Listening Audience of Millions

THE PIONEERING BROADCASTS made in 1906 by Reginald Fessenden from his Brant Rock, MA home had solidified the concept of *broadcasting*. That idea was to distribute entertainment and news from central radio stations, to gather *listeners in the surrounding area* who would remain "tuned-in" as an audience. It was AT & T that came up with the idea of *selling broadcast time for* paid commercial announcements by sponsors.

The formation of broadcasting companies was seen as necessary to raise the capital needed to reach a larger and larger audience, which would serve as a supporting consumer base. Many experimenters created their own businesses, including Fessenden's "National Electric Signaling Company."

Most of these corporations however, did not survive for very long with the exception of the "Marconi Wireless Telegraph Company of America" [1](American Marconi). That company would eventually become the Radio Corporation of America RCA) on November 10, 1919 when American Marconi sold off all of its assets.

To compete with RCA (which was then a subsidiary of General Electric), Westinghouse Broadcasting entered the market, looking for sales of its radio sets and products.

On October 27, 1920 the U.S. Department of Commerce granted Westinghouse a permit to broadcast in Pittsburgh,PA under the radio call letters KDKA. That began the first commercial radio broadcast in the United States, starting on November 2, 1920, to report the results of that year's presidential election.

They used a hand-wound phonograph to play music over the air to fill the times between election returns. KDKA would prove to be a very successful broadcasting station as a result of superior Westinghouse equipment that was developed through acquisition of the patents of Edwin H. Armstrong and Michael Pupin. Rather than compete with Westinghouse, General Electric (GE), Radio Corporation of America (RCA), and American Telephone & Telegraph (AT&T) formed a "patent pool" alliance with the company on June 30, 1921. Between them, they owned every patent dealing with "radio" in America at that time.

While Westinghouse, GE, and RCA primarily focused on the indirect profits of broadcasting which would result from producing and selling radio receivers to the general public, AT&T focused on finding a way of making direct profit from broadcasts.

How "Commercials" Began. AT&T created the concept of "toll broadcasting" which allowed anyone to use a licensed AT&T radio station to broadcast any message of its choosing. Customers would be charged a fee based on when they wanted to purchase time (certain times during the day were more valuable), and how long they wished to be on the air. It was from this concept that the idea of selling blocks of time to commercial advertisers to fund broadcasts was born.

The first such "radio toll station" was WBAY (later consolidated with WEAF) in New York City and it went into operation on July 25, 1922. (Later, it became WNBC.)

Westinghouse, GE, RCA, and AT&T had all become quite successful, so the federal government became interested in their dominance of broadcasting. Members of Congress were worried about the concentration of power these broadcasting companies held, especially because it involved control of the flow of information.

On March 3, 1923 the Federal Trade Commission (FTC) opened an investigation into the radio industry to find out if violations of anti-trust laws were being committed. In its *Report of the Federal Trade Commission on the Radio Industry*, the FTC filed a formal complaint with Congress that Westinghouse, GE, RCA, and AT&T had "combined and conspired for the purpose of restraining competition and creating a monopoly in the manufacture, purchase and sale in interstate commerce of radio receiving devices...and in domestic and transoceanic communication and broadcasting."

Congressional hearings on that matter began in May 1924. Meanwhile, disputes between Westinghouse, GE, RCA, and AT&T led to a shift in power. AT&T was forced out of broadcasting. The survivors formed the National Broadcasting Company (NBC). RCA owned 50%, GE got 30% and Westinghouse 20%.

U.S. Radio Networks. The National Broadcasting Company began regular broadcasting in 1926, using telephone audio links between radio stations in New York and other Eastern cities. NBC became the dominant Radio company, splitting into the "Red and Blue" networks. Despite the earlier power shift, AT&T had maintained its ability to share patents with Westinghouse, GE, and RCA. This led to the Justice Department filing an anti-trust suit against the four companies in May 1930. To avoid trial, AT&T withdrew from the patent pool in 1931 and the remaining three companies developed their own separation plans, *so RCA became the sole owner of NBC.*

A Federal Communications Commission decision in 1939 required NBC to sell its Blue Network. That ruling was sustained by the Supreme Court in a 1943 decision, National Broadcasting Company versus United States, which established the powerful concept that the "scarcity" of radio-frequency spectrum meant broadcasting was subject to more regulation than other media! This gave the U.S. government regulatory power over radio! The sold Blue Network became the American Broadcasting Company (ABC) in 1946.

8

(1927) Philo T. Farnsworth, The U.S. Pioneer of Electronic Television

THE TRUE INVENTOR of television in the United States was Philo T. Farnsworth, the genius son of a Rigby, Idaho, Midwest farming family. In 1920, he explained his invention to his high school science teacher and gave him a drawing that revealed the essentials of his invention. He was then 14. (Years later, that dated drawing, presented by his teacher, won a major patent suit for Farnsworth.)

Farnsworth had invented *raster scanning*, the process of breaking up an image into a series of lines, then "reading" those lines as discrete bits of light and dark areas. If displayed on a cathode ray tube, the lines would assemble "a picture" as the eye connected the light and dark bits into an image. Changing the lines images would cause the image to move. This raster-display system created black-and-white TV.

Farnsworth produced TV cameras and receiving apparatus from 1938 to 1951 in Fort Wayne, Indiana. He was awarded many patents covering TV scanning, contrast, focusing, synchronizing, controls and power. He also invented the first cold-cathode ray tubes, and he used radio waves to get direction (radar), and black light for night vision. His last two patents were for a fusion reactor. At his death in 1971, he had over 300 U.S. and foreign patents. The U.S. honored him in 1983 with a stamp bearing his portrait.

Though Farnsworth was a genius of electronics, he could not compete against the "business tactics" of David Sarnoff (then head of RCA, the surviving company that then held virtually all radio patents and wanted control over TV). Sarnoff had a hired team of scientists, led by Vladimir Zworkin, working on ways to get around the Farnsworth patents. They could not, so Sarnoff had to offer to pay for a patent license from the financially strapped Farnsworth. But fate intervened and World War II began, with the bombing of Pearl Harbor.

The government ordered radio and TV off the air for the war's duration. Farnsworth's television patent expired in six years, just after the war ended. So, his brilliant concept fell into the public domain... and thus, the clutching hands of Sarnoff and RCA.

Monochrome television soon began to vie with Radio to be the big revenue source for broadcasting networks. Although many radio programs continued throughout the decades of the 1950s and 1960s, networks began producing fewer and fewer radio entertainment programs. As radio stopped producing formal fifteen-minute-to hourly shows, a new format developed. "Top 40 music programs" were based on a continuous rotation of short pop music songs presented by a "disc jockey." Famous disc jockeys in the era included Alan Freed, Dick Clark, Don Imus and Wolfman Jack.

Top 40 playlists were theoretically based on record sales; however, record companies began bribing disc jockeys to concentrate their plays on selected artists and songs ... an illegal activity known as *"payola."*

Philo T. Farnsworth was awarded U.S. Patent No. 1,773,980 for his invention of the first fully functional all-electronic television system. Filed on January 7, 1927, and issued on August 26, 1930, this patent detailed his groundbreaking work on the *Image Dissector* (a TV camera) electronic device that converted images into electrical signals. Imagine capturing moving images not with mechanical spinning disks or mirrors, but by harnessing the dance of electrons—was what Farnsworth achieved. His Image Dissector tube was a monumental leap, allowing for the electronic scanning of images, which formed the basis of modern television technology. In a sense, he opened a window to a universe where electronic visuals could be transmitted instantly across vast distances.

Farnsworth's journey wasn't just about innovation; it was also a tale of perseverance. He had to defend his work against giants like RCA and Vladimir Zworykin, who were also racing to develop electronic television. Despite the fierce competition, Farnsworth's clarity of vision and relentless pursuit secured his place in history.

It's astonishing to think how his early 20th-century invention paved the way for the screens that are now integral to our daily lives—from the TVs in our living rooms to the smartphones in our pockets.

9

(1938) Al Gross Invents The "HandieTalkie," The first Handheld Radio Transmitter-Receiver; It Was The "Grandfather" Of Every Cellular Telephone!

JUST BEFORE WORLD War II broke out, radio amateur and engineer, Irving Al Gross, W8PAL invented a unique, handheld, battery powered "radio transceiver." It was dubbed "the handie-talkie" (HT) and it was some accomplishment for its time! Few electronic parts were miniature back in 1938 ... and it used vacuum tubes. But it was brilliantly meant to be easily carried by a soldier or downed pilot, and it was able to exchange voice communications with aircraft and other stations up to

30 miles away. Gross worked with the Wartime Office of Strategic Services (the predecessor of the CIA) during World War II, and his secret invention was responsible for saving countless lives. The SCR-536 "Handie-Talkie was first produced by Motorola in 1941 and widely used and copied thereafter. When the war ended, Chester Gould (famed creator of the *Dick Tracy* comic strip) is said to have visited Al Gross in his lab. He came away with an idea for a two-way wrist radio his comic-strip detective would use to fight crime. It's also been suggested that Gene Roddenberry might have been inspired by that idea to create the small "communicators" used by the *Enterprise* crew in his legendary TV series: *Star Trek*.

Al Gross went on from his ingenious handheld radio creation to develop cordless telephones and pocket paging systems. His efforts also inspired the millions of personal cell phones that would come later. For his lifetime achievements, he was honored by Massachusetts Institute of Technology with the MIT Lemelson Award in 2000. When you next use your cell phone, you'll experience what he alone thought possible nearly a century ago. His invention was the great grandfather of all future pocket cell phones! (Thanks, Al, and 73.)

10

(1942) Hedy Lamarr Invents "Spread Spectrum" To Keep Our WW II Torpedoes on Target. Later, It Becomes CDMA in Our Cellular Phones!

She was an attractive, famous movie star during World War II years. Hedy Lamarr was born Hedwig Eva Maria Kiesler in Vienna, Austria in 1914, and emigrated to the United States, where she became a naturalized American citizen and was signed as an actress by movie mogul, Louis B. Mayer. But she was also an inventor. Lamarr learned (from her boyfriend, Howard Hughes), that radio-controlled torpedoes in use by the U.S. Navy had a vulnerability: their receivers could be jammed by an interfering radio signal, sending the torpedo off course.

Loving a challenge, she came up with a brilliant "timed, frequency-shifting system." It changed the guidance-signal radio frequency at intervals and also automatically retuned the torpedo receiver to each new frequency. Thus, the torpedo received an uninterrupted signal. This thwarted any enemy attempt to jam the signal, since the jammer could not know each new frequency to which the signal had shifted.

Lamarr was assisted in developing her invention by her friend, composer and pianist, George Antheil. Together, they built a working model, using a miniature player-piano mechanism to control the radio signal frequency shifting. They patented it in 1942. But wartime military security kept the invention a secret. Their patent expired and fell into the public domain in 1959. But this ingenious solution endures today. *Spread spectrum* technology is still used in cellular phone networks (as CDMA), as well as in public service radio, Bluetooth and Wi-Fi systems to ensure privacy of communication. It is the modern form of the brilliant system invented by this remarkable woman and her partner, amd was issued U.S. Patent 2,292,387.

11

(1942) How ENIAC, The First "1-and-0" Classic Electronic Digital Computer, Came About

THE U.S. ARMY needed "a good calculation device." It was World War II and America was at war, fighting enemies everywhere. Often, fierce battles raged near homes and villages of innocent civilians and their children. The military faced challenges in accurately calculating artillery trajectories and ranges, to precisely hit enemy targets. This involved solving complex mathematical equations and it was hard, time-consuming and prone to human error when done manually. AT&T's Bell Labs, in New York City had become a "think tank" for the U.S. government in 1940, consulting and developing engineered and innovative solutions to technical problems.

George Stibitz worked there. He was a mathematician, engineer and inventor. He had much expertise in electromechanical relay circuits and in Boolean logic. This made him ideal to tackle the challenge of "calculating utmost accuracy in range-setting to prevent civilian casualties." Mechanical devices were too crude and just wouldn't do, the Army brass said, when visiting Bell Labs. The Army stated its need for precise calculation of huge numbers of artillery range settings, to the very highest accuracy possible.

Stibitz listened carefully. He'd done this sort of thing before. Experimenting with relays at home, on his kitchen table, George had devised an "adder" that used groupings of *binary numbers 1 and 0* to represent regular numbers. His binary adder device showed how the two states: (1) on) and (0) off of electrical switches (or relays) could represent regular numbers in binary notation. Simply by increasing the total amount of binary number "positions," he could represent (code) any regular number in its "binary" form; then, add to it another number written in its binary form; get the answer in binary code, then be instantly decoded to the regular number it represented. It sounds like a lot of work, but at "relay-speed" it took next to no time at all!

Simple, ingenious and fun. Here's an example: Add 2 + 3. In binary, that's 0100 + 1100. That equals binary: 1010 = 5. How? The position of each binary number, moving right, represents a regular number that doubles the one to its left. So, in the above examples, the binary positions represent: **1 2 4 8.** When I turn a position "on", (a 1), the regular number of that place "adds." If I leave it "off," nothing is added. So, 1010 becomes 1 + 0 + 4 + 0, and that's "5" in our regular world. (Now you know how a "classic 1-0" digital computer works!)

George took his invention into the labs. His team liked it. Ideas flowed. The little device became larger and more versatile, and pretty soon, Bell Labs was making and selling *Relay Binary Digital Computer Machines* (all "classic 1-0" types.) He next made a relay computing machine called the *Complex Number Calculator*. It used electromechanical relays and could be operated locally, or from far-away, using a teletype machine that sent data and control keystrokes over wire lines. (So, George Stibitz actually invented the future of networked computing, too.) But, he also "knew his stuff" in electronics...that the "1-and-0" binary states could make use of *much-faster-acting vacuum tubes.* (When a tube's conducting, it's "on." And when it's not, it's "off.") So,

George Stibitz suggested to the Army that it would do better to get "an electronic, vacuum tube, binary digital computer." The Army listened and quickly circulated a request for proposals and bids.

George Stibitz knew his idea would work much faster if electronics was used instead of slower, electromechanical relays. He proposed that the "one-and-zero" binary states could be represented by vacuum tubes. When conducting current, a tube would be "on" or (1). And, when not conducting, it'd be "off" or (0). It would be lots faster than a relay device. So, Stibitz suggested that a vacuum tube, binary electronic digital computer was just what the Army really needed. His thinking not only addressed the immediate wartime need, but it planted the roots of electronic digital computing that have been with us right to the advanced "classic" computers we use today. The Army listened and sought proposals.

12

(1944) Meet ENIAC: The First Electronic Digital Computer

John Eckert and John Mauchly proposed and won the contract to build the **Electronic Numeric Integrator And Computer,** (**ENIAC**) the very first electronic digital computer. They built it at the Moore School of Engineering, at Pennsylvania State U. and it was first used in 1944 to create the complex artillery tables the U.S. Army sought, and then, in 1945, to do Manhattan Project calculations for Los Alamos Laboratories. (These helped in ending World War II.)

ENIAC was an immense machine. It occupied 15,000 square feet of space, had 17,000 vacuum tubes, and had to be manually programmed, by plugging "patch" cords between as many as 6,000 jacks on its panel, and setting a great many rotary switches to exactly the right positions. This manual programming was done by six, amazing women.

13

The Six Mothers of Digital Computing

ENIAC's brilliant team of six, dedicated women did all of its manual programming. They were: **Betty Holberton, Jean Bartik, Kay McNulty, Marilyn Meltzer, Ruth Lichterman and Frances Spencer.** These women created and practiced detailed manual protocols and procedures to correctly program ENIAC with its thousands of plug-in patch-cords and rotary switches. Their work was arduous, demanding, and It had to be *perfect* on each computing run. Had they made errors, ENIAC would have crashed much more often (as it was, vacuum tubes failed often so it crashed almost daily). Too much down-time might have caused the Army to cancel and write-off the electronic digital computer as "a waste of time and unreliable." But thanks to the care and diligent work of the six ENIAC women, electronic digital computing survived! They paved the way to inspire stored-program and naturallanguage programming. But their great gift was keeping the concept of the Electronic Digital Computer alive to grow, prosper and serve us all. Well-done, ladies!

ENIAC had a Profound Impact On Modern Computing. Though massive (15,000 sq. ft.) and challenging to manually program, ENIAC's legacy was as a trailblazer for the advanced classic "1-and-0" computers in use today. It marked the transition from manual to automated digital electronic computation, revolutionizing how we Americans—and now the world—approach and solve problems. It began here in America, and it was a foundational milestone in the evolution of U.S. electronics. It helped lead us to Quantum Computing and Artificial Intelligence. ENIAC is a museum-piece today, but its legacy continues in every digital device. ENIAC, and those who programmed it made digital computing possible and inspired the design of every subsequent generation of high-capability digital and quantum computers and electronics.

Next Came Stored-Programming. Naturalized American Physicist John von Neumann proposed the

Stored-Program Computer concept. A software program file of instructions to be carried-out during a run gets written and pre-stored in the digital computer's memory, alongside the data to be run. When executed, the computer steps through the program file's list of tasks, fetches and processes the data quickly, step-by-step.

14

(Late 1940s) EDVAC Comes to Pennsylvania State U. and Introduces John von Neumann's "Stored Programming"

The EDVAC (Electronic Discrete Variable Automatic Computer) was the next star at the Moore School of Engineering, presided over by naturalized American, Hungarian-born physicist John von Neumann. It fulfilled his insight to store a pre-written program file of machine code instructions, right in the computer's memory, alongside the other data to be run. By doing that, when you'd start a "run," that program would tell the computer "what to do next," and the computer would step through the file's listing of tasks, fetches, and operations, process the data, step-by-step, and yield the result.

It was a great step forward, much faster than the arduous manual programming work of the past. What's more, the program could be "pre-flighted," checked and adjusted before a run, to find and fix any errors. That's how von Neumann did it, and it's how we do it today.

15

Other Famous Digital Computers of American Electronics History

These five noteworthy American electronic digital computers followed ENIAC and showcased advancements in architecture that influenced subsequent systems

1. EDVAC: (Electronic Discrete Variable Automatic Computer): Built in the late 1940s, EDVAC was one of the first computers to implement the stored-program concept, significantly improving programming flexibility and efficiency.
2. UNIVAC: (Universal Automatic Computer): Released in 1951, it became the first commercially available computer in the U.S., making computers accessible for business applications and showcasing magnetic tape data storage.

3. IBM 701: Debuting in 1952, this computer introduced floating-point arithmetic and targeted scientific and research applications, earning its nickname "Defense Calculator."
4. MIT Whirlwind: Developed in the late 1940s and early 1950s, Whirlwind was the first real-time computer capable of processing data instantly, paving the way for interactive computing systems.
5. IBM 1401: Introduced in 1959, the 1401 became immensely popular.

16

(1949) Admiral Grace Hopper Teaches Electronic Digital Computers To Read & Understand Code Written in English!

Dr. Grace Hopper, PhD, was a trailblazer in computer science, a mathematician, and a U.S. Navy rear admiral. She developed early computer software programming languages, including COBOL, still in use today. Hopper also worked on the Harvard Mark I computer during World War II and was one of the first to create a *compiler*, simplifying programming by translating English-based instructions into machine code. Her contributions earned her numerous accolades, including the Presidential Medal of Freedom, awarded posthumously. The USS Hopper, a guided-missile destroyer, was named in her honor, reflecting her lasting impact on both technology and the Navy. It is an inspiring legacy of which all Americans can be justly proud.

17

(1950–60) ELECTRONICS BECOMES AN AMERICAN INDUSTRY!

DEVICES BASED ON electronic functions can be divided into two functional groups: analog and digital. A particular device may consist of circuitry that has either, or a mix, of the two circuit types.

Analog Electronics. Most analog electronic devices, such as radio receivers, are constructed from combinations of several types of basic circuits, such as amplifiers, oscillators and the like. Analog circuitry uses a wide range of voltages or currents for its operation as compared to the discrete voltage-level steps used in digital circuitry.

The number of different analog circuits so far devised is quite huge, especially because a 'circuit' can be defined as anything from a single component to systems containing thousands of components.

Analog circuits are sometimes called *linear circuits* although many nonlinear effects can be accomplished in analog circuits, such as amplifiers, mixers, and modulators. Good examples of analog circuits include vacuum tube and transistor amplifiers, as well as operational and radio frequency amplifiers and oscillators.

Digital Electronics. It's a field of electronics involving use of digital devices and the systems that use or produce them. Digital electronic circuits are usually made from large assemblies of transistor logic gates, combined into integrated circuits. Complex devices may have simple electronic representations of Boolean logic functions. The binary number system was developed by Gottfried Leibniz in 1705. He also established that by using the binary system, the principles of arithmetic and logic could be joined. Digital logic as we know and use it today was stated by George Boole in the mid-19th century.

18

(1947–1956) Drs. John Bardeen, Walter Brattain and William Shockley Invent The Point-Contact Transistor At Bell Labs. Then, They Receive The 1956 Nobel Prize In Physics

In 1947, just before the mid-twentieth century, new and revolutionary solid-state *semiconductor* technology appeared. The *transistor* (named by Dr. John Pierce, head of New York's Bell Labs) exploded into technology and changed the world forever. The three physicist-geniuses who had worked under his direction agreed that his choice for its name perfectly united both functions of the device: *Trans*fer and Res*istor...transistor!* It quickly found its way into radios and electronic devices, displacing fragile vacuum tubes and creating the solid-state design specialization that brought new ruggedness and long life to electronics, ushering vacuum tubes toward obsolescence.

But, not everywhere. Acceptance of germanium transistors in some applications was slow. Ed Cole, the legendary engineering head and later president of General Motors opposed use of early germanium transistors in cars, for safety reasons. His opposition helped lead to creation of vastly more-rugged *silicon s*emiconductors and the development of MOSFETs (metal oxide semiconductor field-effect transistors.) These were reliable and lowcost...and they led the way to create "integrated circuits" and large-scale integration. In turn, those led to "smartphones" with *millions* of transistors inside and previously undreamed-of capabilities!

When the royals of Sweden conferred the Nobel Prize on these three men in 1956, they presented great gratitude from all the world, both of tomorrow, as well as today.

19

(1953) Color Television Broadcasting Arrives

IN THE 1950S, America's RCA-owned NBC and its competitor, the CBS television network introduced competing technology systems for TV broadcasting in color. The CBS field-sequential system was not at all compatible with black-and white TV receivers, but the RCA technology used by NBC was.

So, the Federal Communications Commission approved it as the first American black-and-white-compatible color television standard, then used by NBC in December 1953.

The first network color-cast followed on January 1, 1954, with NBC transmitting the annual Tournament of Roses Parade in Pasadena, California to over 20 stations across the country.)

20

(1958) Jack S. Kilby Invents the Integrated Circuit at Texas Instruments

Jack St. Clair Kilby is renowned for several groundbreaking inventions that shaped modern electronic technology:

- The "IC" or "Integrated Circuit" (Chip) Kilby invented the first working integrated circuit in 1958 while at Texas Instruments. This innovation revolutionized electronics by enabling the miniaturization of circuits and combining them on the same silicon substrate with active semiconductor devices.
- The Handheld Calculator: He co-invented the first handheld calculator, known as the Texas

Instruments *Pocketronic,* which made complex calculations hand-portable and accessible.

- The Thermal Printer: Kilby also contributed to the development of the thermal printer, an early device that used heat to produce images or text on special paper.

These inventions had a profound impact on all industries ranging from computing to telecommunications. Kilby received the Nobel prize in Physics in 2000 for the IC.

21

(1969) NASA Astronauts Are First To Reach, Land On The Moon And Safely Return

The United States of America is the first country to have successfully conducted crewed missions to the Moon. The heroic *Apollo* 11 achievement first took place on July 20, 1969. Astronaut Neil Armstrong became the first human to walk on the moon and he planted an American flag as proof of our visit. The electronics of the spacecraft was rudimentary and lacked LSI integrated circuits and microelectronics, which were then in their infancy.

The heroic crewmembers were: Neil A. Armstrong, Commander; Michael Collins, Command Module Pilot; Edwin "Buzz" E. Aldrin, Jr., Lunar Module Pilot.

22

(1977) The World Watches as NASA Launches Voyagers 1 and 2 on a Never-Ending Journey to Explore Our 4 Outer Solar System Planets and Interstellar Space

The two Voyager Space Probes were launched separately by NASA on August 20, 1977, during an amazing, rare alignment of the four outer planets of our solar system that occurs only once every 176 years! This maximized the benefits to our probe "flybys" of the planets, provided sensational images, and positively added to the precision of navigation by the now-antique electronics aboard the two spacecraft.

In their 50 years of operation, the two probes have now reached a position in interstellar space some *16 billion miles* from Earth. They will never return, but keep exploring forever. Power has been shut off to non-essential instruments aboard the two craft, so that radio contact can be sustained as long as possible. Each Voyager has a 23-watt transmitter on board and a directional antenna system. It takes about 22 hours for a radio signal from a Voyager probe to be received here on Earth.

23

(1980–88) How Jesse E. Russell Of Bell Labs Invented The 2G Digital Cell Phone Network

As the 1980s arrived, AT&T analog mobile services continued to be deployed as "car phones." The old-tech analog car phones were about the only mobile communications service then available from AT&T and its Bell subsidiaries, and these analog designs had the same old problems. Mobile phone services were implemented in a standardized way on all networks throughout the U.S. so that all phones could work the same way everywhere, no matter the state or city. But, these analog car phone services were just mediocre. Call capacity was a big problem. Being analog radio, there was never enough frequency spectrum available to serve all callers, especially in cities and metropolitan areas. Typically, a city might have twenty-two channels – always in use – so other customers could not make their calls when they needed to. And, operating costs were very high.

So, Bell operating companies and their customers all tried to hand the troublesome analog car phone business back to AT&T. But just then, that corporation was undergoing the eight-year-long legal battle over a court-ordered company breakup that began in 1974. So, it was really busy and preoccupied.

In 1982, the Regional Bell Operating Companies were being formed. So, the car phone problem wasn't first on AT&T's agenda. So, the problem circulated from desk-to-desk at Bell Labs. Finally, in 1988, it landed on the desk of Jesse E. Russell, a brilliant, young, black engineer who'd graduated from Tennessee State and Stanford Universities. He bravely proposed a totally new and exciting solution – go digital!

His solution changed the entire character and future of mobile phones! But, there's more: Jesse Russell wasn't just the digital network engineering genius at AT&T, he was the brilliant guy who proposed taking those cell phones out of the car and putting them into your pocket or purse!

So, the personal phone and digital cellular network he designed made possible digital voice processing and bandwidth-saving. This increased the number of calls that could be shared on each channel. It ranks as a truly monumental engineering achievement that brought cell phones to the forefront of human communication, solved the old analog capacity problem, and allowed new digital data services that simply were not possible with old analog technology.

Russell became an IEEE fellow in 1994 for his technology leadership in wireless communication concepts, systems and standards. In 1999. He was also named a fellow of the IEC. His contribution to every cell phone user has had a phenomenal impact on the rise of personal communication.

24

(1991) IBM Pioneers "Simon," A Highly Advanced, Personal Digital Cellular Phone; (2001); the 3G Digital Network Arrives; and (2007); Apple's iPhone Debuts

IN 1991, IBM patented a cell-phone-like device that was the neat integration of *a personal digital assistant* with *a digital cellular telephone*. By 1994, IBM had commenced marketing its *Simon Personal Communicator.* It was the very first "smart phone." A handheld device with a touchscreen interface, it was meant to do faxes, emails, phones cellular paging, as well as other functions. It came with eleven resident programs, which included an appointment scheduler, clock, sketch and handwritten notepad and calculator, a unique IBM-developed stylus input and keyboard with prediction features, facsimile and onboard modem, as well as 1 megabyte of ROM (read-only memory), 1 megabyte of RAM (random access memory)and a 16-bit (X86) processor.

The three people most responsible for conceiving and creating Simon were engineers Frank J. Canova, Jr., Jerry Merckel and then-head of IBM's Florida Lab, Paul Mugge. It was a brilliant, visionary, pioneering invention. Not only had nothing like Simon ever existed before; what it was capable of doing vastly exceeded the "network technology" then available in the 1990s. It was simply too advanced.

It weighed 510 grams, was powered by a NiCad battery that yielded eight hours of standby, or constant operation of just one hour, and ran on Bellsouth Cellular, over a network that spanned just fifteen of the lower U.S. states. Some 50,000 Simons were sold, at about $900 each. The featured touchscreen could send and receive emails, faxes and texts, had full internet access and allowed web browsing, as if you were at a desktop computer. It was amazing. But the network moxy it needed to succeed did not exist! (Remember dial-up? That was what the internet was like, back then.) So, sales stalled.

Simon only lasted until 1994, and IBM had no choice but to pull the plug.

Digital cellphones continued to do well, but few offered a brilliant gamut of services and capabilities to rival IBM's Simon. So, the notion of a "smartphone" endured a long, thirteen-year hibernation until 2007, when Steve Jobs re-introduced that level of technology in his first Apple iPhone. It incorporated many of the IBM Simon's breathtaking features, but the newly updated network it would be able to runon had, by now, matured enough to provide for them!

Apple iPhone. The Apple iPhone family of handsets was introduced in 2007, with new products debuting every year thereafter. With so many products, it's harder to find truly differentiating *changes* in features and functions. However, the overruling tenet of marketing is that *the product is what the customer thinks it is*. The operating system is Apple's iOS. Things must be going well for Apple, as a company disclosure not long ago said that the company had an income of $1 million every 8.8 minutes, or a tad over $163 million per day! (By the way, Tim Cook, who heads Apple, was formerly an employee at IBM.)

Apple products had been made in China by Foxconn (a Chinese Communist company). Ongoing charges of human rights abuses against the CCP, and Communist leadership of China, as well as suicide stories of Foxconn employees, plus trade friction are among the many reasons leading Apple to announce it will relocate to India and the U.S., spending some $500 billion on new facilities. The reshoring date has not been announced.

Androids. The other class of cellular handsets with multiple manufacturers is Androids. Based on Linux, the operating system. pioneered by inventor Linus Torvald, these handsets have estimable clout because the software system is controlled by Google (or, if you prefer, Alphabet). This company makes $1 million every 17.1 minutes, or $84.2 million per day. Samsung actually produces most of the android handsets. The integrated circuit chips in an android contain as many as *eight billion* tiny transistors. Some say transistors may have been made about as small as they can be, and still be able to function, but new ideas keep coming! Samsung has also announced it will relocate to the U.S. in the future.

25

(1948–1955) Electronic Digital Computers Move From Vacuum Tubes to Transistors

In England, at the University of Manchester, Tom Kilburn, Frederic Williams and Geoff Tootill designed and built the first transistor electronic, stored-program digital computer. It used newly developed American transistors, instead of vacuum tubes.

Called "The Manchester Baby," it had only one kilobit (1024 bits) of memory, ran its first program in June, 1948, was operational by 1953, and a second version was completed in April 1955. From then on, transistors replaced vacuum tubes in computer designs, giving rise to the "second generation" of digital computers.

Compared to vacuum tubes, transistors of the time were much smaller, more reliable, had unlimited lifespans, used far less power, gave off much less heat, and allowed much denser concentrations of circuitry. But there was more to come.

26

(1958) Silicon Transistors and Integrated Circuits Change Electronics

THESE 'LATE-1950S DEVELOPMENTS" forecast the end of the vacuum tube's dominance in American electronics and heralded the coming new solid-state era in 20th century design. By this time, computers had gone over to use of transistors. These were much smaller, required less power, ran cooler, faster and performed almost 1,000 more operations per second than could tube designs. As integrated circuitry and microprocessors came, computers shrank from room-size to desktop, laptop and handheld devices as digital electronics design surged ahead from the 1960s to the 1990s.

27

(1924–1980): The Rise of IBM

Electronics giant IBM was founded in 1911 as C-T-R, a U.S. holding company for three computing, tabulating and recordkeeping machine-makers. Over time, these three companies made calculators, weighing machines, punched-card tabulators, and meat slicers. In 1924 IBM was renamed International Business Machines, but most folks still called it "IBM." (This information has been provided by the Editors of Wikipedia.)

Today, IBM is big and global, with operations in 170 countries. It is primarily known as a research and technology firm with principal products in high-speed electronic computers and related systems. But it constantly innovates.

It got into high-speed electromechanical calculators during WWII. Then, became the pre-eminent choice for Electronic Digital Computers among leaders in business, banking and finance, and it maintained a top-notch position in customer service. Its research work has led to some startling triumphs in physics and material sciences. Employees have collected an impressive array of recognitions and awards for their scientific research and inventions. These include:

Six Nobel Prizes; six Turing Awards; Ten National Medals of Technology; and five National Medals of Science.

IBM Fellows have generated over 9,329 patents, thousands of government and professional citations, and have a massive store of published research in scientific journals worldwide. IBM Research is the largest industrial research organization in the world and has 12 labs on six continents. An echo of our 1969 “Eagle” landing on the Moon was IBM’s “Eagle” Quantum Computer, a 127-Qubit processor that IBM unveiled in 2021 amid claims that it could not be simulated by any classical computer. Just ahead are photonic switching devices that can be made smaller than a transistor no wider than a strand of DNA, and so, do not have their “Heisenberg Uncertainty Principle” problems. (Micro transistors can exhibit “tunnelling” and other effects that stop their transistor action due to quantum mechanics) and keep the electrons from flowing as they should, Work continues on new tech devices that use light and electron spins. And watch for the stunning breakthrough in fault-tolerant quantum computing, coming by 2029! Stay tuned for more details as technology marches on.

28

(1981) The IBM Personal Computer Arrives

BACK IN 1981, IBM had just awoken to the new thought that home and personal computers were 'real' products. So, the management of IBM was quite late getting into this business area, because so many in the company had thought these small systems were just "toys for hobbyists" and not "serious computers for business." How wrong they were!

The company formed a small group in Boca Raton, FL, headed by Phillip Don Estridge and tasked with coming up with a personal computer offering. Ordinarily, IBM would have developed and built the major components of such a product. But, their late start foreclosed that path. The only choice open to them now was to buy "off-the-shelf" components, and this would later prove a fatal wound to the late-stage IBM PC.

IBM had made nothing but "mainframe" computers for years. Its people, the IBM culture, and DNA knew only "big" computers. So, small computers were new and strange to the IBMers who had made System 360, 370 and other classic IBM mainframes the choice of governments and big businesses everywhere.

So, mostly ignored or neglected by co-workers, the IBM PC hardware was readied by the small Boca Raton workgroup in less than a year! Now it was time to find an operating system to run it.

This is a tale of misfortune unequalled in technology history.

In 1982, IBM's tech staff went far afield in search of a software operating system for the IBM PC. They contacted many on their short list of "people who might know someone." But, beng IBM, they required that everyone they spoke with sign a "nondisclosure agreement." This meant that no signer could ever tell anyone, whom they had spoken with, nor the subject they'd spoken about, under threat of being sued.

Back then, Bill Gates, (now, the billionaire from Microsoft) was just a 26-year-old college-dropout. He had provided the IBM seekers with Gary Kildall's name, address and phone number. Kildall was a genius computer scientist when few existed.

So, the IBMers soon showed up at the home of the Kildalls, Gary and Dorothy, who were a married couple. Their residence was also the address of "Digital Research Co.", a startup software company with just a single product: **CP/M,** a software *control product for microcomputers.*

Gary was a master developer... and a pilot. He had flown his small light plane out that day to deliver a new software package to a customer. He was due back that afternoon. When IBM showed up on the doorstep with the nondisclosure agreement, Gary's wife, Dorothy called their lawyer, who advised her not to sign until Gary had seen and okayed the agreement.

The IBMers, visibly annoyed, agreed to return later. Earlier, Bill Gates, who had previously signed IBM's non-disclosure, had placed a phone call to Gary and left the cryptic message that "some very important people are coming to see you." But, due to having signed the NDA, he could say no more.

Gary returned later that day and one may assume that Dorothy told him as much as she could. The IBMers also came back. Gary still refused to sign. But, he left with them. Negotiations continued. They offered Gary a flat $250,000, one-time payment for outright purchase of CP/M. But Gary did not wish to sell it, saying he preferred a royalty arrangement.

Meanwhile, his client. Seattle Computer Products (SCP), had earlier developed an 8086 board product it wanted to market and had contracted with Kildall for a modified version of CP/M to run on it. Delivery had now become very, very late and SCP's sales were being hurt. So, a young employee of SCP modified CP/M to make "QDOS 0.11" and called it: Quick and Dirty Operating System. It began shipping in September 1980. It was said to have been more formally named "86-DOS" by SCP in December 1980.

The hearsay tale is told that CP/M became "QDOS"and might have become 86-DOS. Gates acquired the rights to "86-DOS," paying SCP $75,000. The story goes on to say that Gates renamed his purchase "Microsoft DOS" and then contacted the IBMers to offer it for use in the IBM PC. Since the legal "rights" of software ownership had not then been fully developed, Gary Kildall believed he had no legal recourse. But the hearsay was that CP/M had been ripped-off. When he protested this to IBM, the firm said it would offer his CP/M software to its PC customers as an alternative to Microsoft DOS. It did so, for the price of $240. Right next to it was Microsoft DOS, priced at $40...one-sixth the price! Kildall lost out again.

This tale has been retold for years. It underscores the point that one cannot be too careful in making big decisions and to persevere in getting good advice.

Meanwhile, sales of the IBM Personal Computer vastly exceeded every financial projection ever made by IBM. Its actual sales were said to be 800% higher than IBM's estimates!

In 2009, IBM acquired software company SPSS Inc. and later in 2009, IBM's Blue Gene supercomputing program was awarded the National Medal of Technology and Innovation. And, the IBM PC was still an unqualified success! But, then, an untold flood of "cloning" hit, as many competitors swamped the industry with "clones" of the PC. By identifying every off-the-shelf component used in the IBM PC, competitors could readily identify *the component sources and buy the same parts*. Then, it was just a simple matter of manufacturing, to assemble their own duplicates (clones) of the IBM PC. The flood of clones deluged the market, many from offshore makers, and drove down prices.

Though the IBM PC had sold well for a number of years, giving IBM 25% of the market, with sales of nearly a million units at one point in the 1990s, profitability suffered for the IBM PC as clone-makers dropped their prices in a frenzy of selling as the market fell. Meanwhile, hearsay said several clone software makers had also "reverse-engineered" MS DOS, so there was an abundance of CP/M look-alike software from other suppliers.

As sales of the IBM PC plummeted in the flood of clones, IBM exited the PC market and sold its PC business to the Chinese company, Lenovo, on May 1, 2005. (In recent years, Lenovo has become the #1 PC seller in the world.)

29

(1976) Apple Computer Springs From Electronic Hobby Interest... In A Garage!

(Information has been provided by the Editors of Wikipedia.) Though originally named Apple Computer, Inc., Apple is now a multinational corporation that creates and markets consumer electronics and computer software, It is also a digital distributor of media content. Apple's core product lines are the iPhone smartphone, iPad tablet computer, and the Macintosh personal computer. The company offers its products online and has a chain of retail stores known as Apple Stores.

Founders Steve Jobs, Steve Wozniak, and Ronald Wayne created Apple Computer Co. on April 1, 1976, to market Wozniak's Apple desktop computer, and Jobs and Wozniak incorporated the company on January 3, 1977, in Cupertino, California.

For more than three decades, Apple Computer was predominantly a manufacturer of personal computers, including the Apple II, Macintosh, and Power Mac but it faced rocky sales and low market share during the 1990s. Jobs, who had been ousted from the company in 1985, returned to Apple in 1997 after his company,

NeXT, was bought by Apple. The following year he became the company's interim CEO, and later, it became permanent. Jobs subsequently instilled a new corporate philosophy of recognizable products and simple design, starting with the original iMac in 1998.

With the introduction of the successful iPod music player in 2001 and iTunes Music Store in 2003, Apple established itself as a leader in the consumer electronics and media sales industries, leading it to drop the word: "Computer" from the company's name in 2007. The company is also known for its iOS range of smart phones, media players, and tablet computer products that began with the iPhone, followed by the iPod Touch and then the iPad.

As of June 30, 2015, Apple was the largest publicly traded corporation in the world by market capitalization, with an estimated value of US $1 trillion as of August 2, 2018. Apple's worldwide annual revenue in 2010 totaled US$65 billion, growing to US $127.8 billion in 2011and $156 billion in 2012.

Steve Jobs and Steve Wozniak first met in mid-1971, when their mutual friend Bill Fernandez introduced the 21-year-old Wozniak to the 16-year-old Jobs. Their business partnership began in the fall of that year when Wozniak, a self-educated electronics engineer, read an article in *Esquire* magazine that described a device that could place free, long-distance phone calls, by emitting specific tone chirps. Wozniak started to build his original "blue boxes. Jobs managed to sell some two hundred blue boxes for $150 each and split the profit with Wozniak. Jobs later said that if it hadn't been for Wozniak's blue boxes, "there wouldn't have been an Apple."

By 1972, Jobs had withdrawn from Reed College and Wozniak from UC Berkeley. The two started attending meetings of the Homebrew Computer Club. New microcomputers such as the Altair 8800 and the IMSAI 8080 inspired Wozniak to build a microprocessor into his video terminal circuit, to make a complete computer. At the time the only microcomputer CPUs generally available were the $179 Intel 8080 (equivalent to $973+ now), and the then-$170 Motorola 6800 CPU chip (equivalent to $925+ now). Wozniak preferred the 6800, but both were out of his price range. So, he watched, and learned, and designed computers on paper, waiting for the day he could afford a CPU.

When MOS Technology released its $20 (equivalent to $103+ now) 6502 chip in 1976, Wozniak wrote a version of BASIC for it, and then began to design a computer for it to run on. The 6502 was designed by the same people who designed the 6800, as many in Silicon Valley had left earlier employers to form their own companies.

So, Wozniak's earlier 6800 "computer-on-paper" needed only minor changes to run on the new chip! By March 1, 1976, Wozniak completed the machine and took it to a Homebrew Computer Club meeting to show it off. When Jobs saw Wozniak's computer (which later became the Apple I), he was immediately interested in its commercial potential. Initially, Wozniak had intended to share schematics of the machine for free, but Jobs insisted that they should build and sell bare printed circuit boards for the computer. Wozniak originally offered the design to Hewlett-Packard (HP), where he worked at the time, but his offer was denied by the company on *five* occasions. (There is a great object lesson here, to make decisions that fully consider the future potential of any seemingly-unusual innovation. Wozniak's design began Apple, and it grew to become the world's foremost company, based on market capitalization.) Back to our story.

Jobs eventually convinced Wozniak to go into business together and start a new company of their own. In order to raise the money they needed to produce the first batch of printed circuit boards, Jobs sold his Volkswagen Type 2 minibus for a few hundred dollars, and Wozniak his HP-65 programmable calculator for $500.

Steve Jobs' parents' home in Los Altos, California, was where Apple started its operation. Initial work took place in his bedroom and later moved to the home's garage. Wozniak's Apple I design was sold as an assembled circuit board and lacked basic features such as a keyboard, monitor, and case.

On April 1, 1976, Apple Computer Company was founded by Steve Jobs, Steve Wozniak, and Ronald Wayne. The company was registered as a California business partnership. Wayne, who worked at Atari as a chief draftsman, became a co-founder in return for a 10% stake. On April 12, less than two weeks after the company's formation, Wayne left Apple, selling his 10% share back to the two Steves for $800.

According to Wozniak, Jobs proposed the name "Apple Computer" when he had just come back from one of his fruitarian diets, when he conceived of the name and thought "it sounded fun, spirited and not intimidating ... plus, it would get us ahead of Atari in the phone book."

The two Steves made a last trip to the Homebrew Computer Club and demonstrated the Apple I. Paul Terrell, who operated the computer store chain *Byte Shop*, was impressed, and gave the two Steves his card, asking them to keep in touch. The next day, Jobs visited Terrell at the Mountain View Byte Shop store, and tried to sell him the bare circuit boards for the Apple I. Terrell said he was only interested in purchasing the machine fully assembled, and that he would order 50 assembled computers and pay $500 each on delivery (equivalent to $2,600+ now). Jobs took the purchase order from the Byte Shop to national electronic parts distributor Cramer Electronics, and ordered the components needed. When asked by the credit manager how he would pay for the parts, Jobs replied, "I have this purchase order from the Byte Shop chain of computer stores for 50 of my computers and the payment terms are COD. If you give me the parts on net 30-day terms I can build and deliver the computers in that time frame, collect my money from Terrell at the Byte Shop and pay you."

The two Steves and their small crew spent day and night building and testing the computers and made delivery to Terrell on- time. The Apple I went on sale in July 1976 as an assembled circuit board with a retail price of $666.66 About 200 units of the Apple I were eventually sold.

It had some notable features, including a TV display, whereas many machines of the time had no display at all. It was not like the displays of later machines; the text was displayed at 60 characters per second – still faster than the teleprinters of contemporary machines of that era. The machine had bootstrap code on ROM, making it easier to start up. At the insistence of Paul Terrell, Wozniak designed a cassette interface for loading and saving programs, at the then-rapid pace of 1200 bits per sec. The simple machine was a masterpiece of design using far fewer parts than anything in its class and earned Wozniak a reputation as a designer.

Jobs looked for investments to expand the business, but banks were reluctant to lend money; the idea of a computer for ordinary people seemed absurd at the time. In August 1976, Jobs approached his former boss at Atari, Nolan Bushnell, who recommended that he meet with Don Valentine, the founder of Sequoia Capital. Valentine was not interested in funding Apple, but he introduced Jobs to Mike Markkula, a millionaire who had worked with him at Fairchild Semiconductor. Markkula saw great potential in the two Steves, and became an angel investor of their company. He invested $92,000 in Apple out of his own property while securing a $250,000 line of credit from Bank of America. In return, Markkula received a onethird stake in Apple. Apple Computer, Inc. became incorporated on January 3, 1977. The new corporation bought out the partnership the two Steves had formed nine months earlier.

In February 1977, Markkula recruited Michael Scott from National Semiconductor to serve as the first president and CEO of Apple Computer, as the two Steves were both insufficiently experienced and he was not interested in taking that position himself. That same month, Wozniak resigned from his job at Hewlett-Packard to work full-time for Apple.

He moved on from the Apple I and began designing a greatly improved computer: the Apple II. (Ed. Note: I had an Apple II Plus.) Wozniak completed a working prototype of the new machine by August 1976. The two Steves presented the Apple II computer to the public at the first West Coast Computer Faire on April 16 and 17, 1977. In the May 1977 issue of *Byte*,. Wozniak said of the Apple II design, "To me, a personal computer should be small, reliable, convenient to use, and inexpensive."

The Apple II went on sale on June 10, 1977, with a retail price of $1,298. The computer's main internal difference from its predecessor was a completely redesigned TV interface, which held the display in memory. Now not only useful for simple text display, the Apple II included graphics and, eventually, color. During the development of the Apple II, Jobs pressed for a well-designed plastic case and built-in keyboard, with the idea that the machine should be fully packaged and ready to run out of the box. This was almost the case for the Apple I computers, but one still needed to plug various parts together and type in the code to run BASIC. Jobs wanted the Apple II case to be "simple and elegant", and hired an industrial designer (Jerry Manock) to produce such a case design. Apple employee #5. Rod Holt, developed the switching power supply.

While early Apple II models used ordinary cassette tapes as storage devices, they were superseded in 1978 by the introduction of a 5-1/4-inch floppy disk drive and interface called the Disk II. The Disk II system was designed by Wozniak and released with a retail price of $495.

In 1979, the Apple II was chosen to be the desktop platform for the first, new, "killer application" of the business world: *VisiCalc,* a spreadsheet program. This was so important that the Apple II became what was described as a "VisiCalc accessory."

The software application created a business market for the Apple II Computer and gave home users an additional reason to buy it: their compatibility with the office.

Before VisiCalc, Apple had been a distant third place competitor to Commodore and Tandy. The Apple II was one of the three "1977" computers generally credited with creating the home computer market (the other two being the Commodore PET and the Tandy Corporation TRS-80). A number of different models of the Apple II were built thereafter, including the Apple II-plus, the Apple IIe. (My wife and I raised two brilliant, techie sons on these). Then came the Apple IIGS, which was established as a successful, business-ready platform, because of VisiCalc. But, Apple management was not content. The Apple III was conceived and designed to take on the business environment in an attempt to compete with IBM in the business and corporate computing market. The development of the Apple III started in late 1978 and was subsequently developed by a committee headed by Jobs. The Apple III was first announced on May 19, 1980, with a retail price ranging from $4,340 to $7,800, and it was released in November 1980. It was a failure.

On December 12, 1980, Apple (ticker symbol "AAPL") went public selling 4.6 million shares at $22 per share ($.10 per share when adjusting for stock splits as of November 30, 2020), generating over $100 million, which was more capital than any IPO since Ford Motor Company in 1956. Several venture capitalists cashed out, reaping billions in long-term capital gains. By the end of the day, the stock rose to $29 per share and 300 millionaires were created, including the two Steves. Around this time Wozniak offered $10 million of his own stock to early Apple employees. Apple's market cap was $1.778 billion at the end of its first day of trading. By August 1981 Apple was among the three largest microcomputer companies, having replaced Radio Shack as the leader; revenue in the first half of the year had already exceeded 1980's $118 million, and *InfoWorld* reported that lack of production capacity was constraining growth. Because of VisiCalc, businesses purchased 90% of Apple IIs; large customers especially preferred Apple.

IBM entered the personal computer market in 1981 with the IBM PC in part because it did not want products without IBM logos on customers' desks, but Apple had many advantages. While IBM began with one microcomputer, little available hardware or software, and a couple of hundred dealers, Apple had five times as many dealers in the US and an established international distribution network. The Apple II had an installed base of more than 250,000 customers, and hundreds of independent developers offered software and peripherals; at least ten databases and ten word processors were available, while the IBM PC had zero databases and a single word processor. By 1984, the two companies were rivals, but IBM had $4 billion in annual PC revenue, more than twice that of Apple. A survey found that 56% of American companies with personal computers used IBM PCs, compared to 16% for Apple. Small businesses, schools, and homes became the Apple II's primary market.

By early 1985, the Macintosh's failure to defeat the IBM PC triggered a power struggle between Jobs and CEO John Sculley. Sculley favored open architecture computers like the Apple II, sold to education, small business, and home markets, which were less vulnerable to IBM. Jobs wanted the company to focus on closed architecture Macintosh, as a business alternative to the IBM PC.

As president and CEO, Sculley, had little control over Chairman Jobs' Macintosh division, so it and the Apple II division operated like completely separate companies. Though its products provided 85% of Apple's sales, the company's January 1985 annual meeting did not mention the Apple II division or its employees. This frustrated Wozniak, who left Apple in the spring of that year, and sold most of his stock. Despite his grievances, Wozniak left the company amicably and remained an Apple shareholder following his departure.

In April 1985, Sculley decided to remove Jobs as the general manager of the Macintosh division, and gained unanimous support from the Apple board of directors. Rather than submit to Sculley's direction, Jobs attempted to oust him from Apple. An emergency executive meeting was held, where Apple's executive staff sided with Sculley and stripped Jobs of all operational duties. Jobs, taking the position of Chairman of the Board had no influence over Apple's direction and resigned in September 1985, taking a number of Apple employees with him to found NeXT Inc. In a show of defiance at being set aside by Apple Computer, Jobs sold all but one of his 6.5 million shares in the company for $70 million.

Despite its initial marketing difficulties, the Macintosh brand was eventually a success for Apple, due to its introduction of desktop publishing (and later computer animation) through Apple's partnership with Adobe Systems, which introduced the laser printer. and Adobe PageMaker. The Macintosh became the platform of choice for work in many arts industries, including cinema, music, advertising, packaging and publishing.

30

(1980–2024) IBM Fields the Powerful Category of Classic "SuperComputers"

IBM introduced a number of "supercomputers" throughout the 20th century, beginning with the custom-built tabulators it made for Columbia University in 1954. However, that word gained a lot in expressing "power" when it was discovered that multiple processors could be used to solve a problem, working in parallel.

It began in the 1980s with computers using only a few processors. But, by the 1990s, machines with thousands of processors began appearing in the U.S. and Japan. These set new performance records. By the end of the 20th century, massively parallel supercomputers with thousands of processors (such as those used in personal computers) were in use.

By 2010, dramatic power was achieved by supercomputers using over 60,000 processors. Performance at the *petaflop* level was achieved. (A petaflop is one-quadrillion floating-point operations per second.)

But, these computers were still of the *classic variety.* That is, they used binary logic and represented numbers using binary "1s" and "0s," so they had those same weaknesses. There were still problems they could not solve. The impressive history rolled-up by Cray *Titan* and IBM supercomputers, through *Sequoia*, IBM's thirdgeneration Blue-Gene system of 2012, achieved then-unheard-of speeds as high as *16.32 petaflops*.

But these huge supercomputers still had to plod through *one solution at a time* to solve problems like picking an optimal path to visit several destinations. Also, there were still problems that could not readily be solved by classic "1s-and-0s" computer processing.

31

(1998): Quantum Computers Arrive

According to the editors of Wikipedia.org, a consulting firm in 1998 early expressed a view that "investment dollars were pouring in, and quantum-computing start-ups were proliferating." However, actual progress in developing functional quantum computers then was being made only by a few firms and researchers. The actual evolution of quantum computers is an intriguing subject that began with their theoretical groundwork, laid down in the 20th century, as summarized below. However, there has been much, continuing evolution. Here's a timeline:

1920s: Modern quantum theory was developed, to explain wave-particle duality observed at atomic scales.

1980: Paul Benioff described the first quantum mechanical model of a computer, demonstrating that computation could be performed according to quantum mechanical principles.

1981: At the inaugural Conference on *Physics of Computation*, Paul Benioff and Richard Feynman presented lectures on quantum computing. Feynman's talk underlined the "inefficiency of simulating quantum systems on classical computers" and suggested a model for a true *quantum computer*.

1985: David Deutsch introduced the expanded concept of *a universal quantum computer,* providing a theoretical basis for quantum computation.

1994: Peter Shor developed "Shor's algorithm," which enables a quantum computer to factor large numbers significantly faster than the very best classical algorithms.

1998: Isaac Chuang, Neil Gershenfeld, and Mark Kubinec created the first 2-qubit quantum computer, capable of data processing and solution output.

Since then, quantum computing has experienced very rapid development, with substantial investments from both governments and private sources. The challenges have been decoherence, noise and error rates. The ultimate goal is to develop scalable quantum computers, capable of performing specific computations exponentially faster than their classical (0 and 1) counterparts.

While it is emerging from the experimental phase, quantum computing now has great potential for widespread applications, including breaking encryption, handling large number problems, and dealing with complex physical simulations.

One of the most difficult problems of quantum computers is *noise.* It comes from very many sources and it causes errors. Increasing the number of qubits has helped, quite a bit. Other methods are being tried and new chip concepts have improved noise factors. Now, IBM has stated, that in 2029, we will see arrival of a truly "fault-tolerant" design with 20,000 times better performance than the best system now. IBM is a formidable predictor, but time will tell.

32

What Sort of Problems Can You Tackle With A Quantum Computer?

Answer: Anything that requires complex, repetitive calculations, because there are so many possible outcomes. Now, keep the following analogy in mind of the difference between classic and quantum computer types: in finding a solution, a classic "0 and 1" computer will *"flip a coin"* one-at-a-time, in order to arrive at one out of many possible answers. It must do that "spin" for *every possible choice that exists* and that can take a *very, very* long time!

A quantum computer works differently. Instead of flipping a coin, it *"spins a coin on its edge!"* And so, it can reveal *all possible outcomes in one spin!* So, the answer comes lots *faster*!

Now, remember, these are *analogies*. Nothing actually flips or spins in either of these computer types. But these are descriptive of the different ways they work. My aim is for you to see the massive difference in processing time between them. It can take *years* for a classic computer to do a *gazillion* runs, one-at-a-time, as it attempts to find a good answer...which might not even be possible. Meanwhile, the same problem might be solved in *microseconds*, as a quantum computer reveals all possible results in *one* run.

To give you an example, here is one of the most difficult, yet simple-seeming problems. It is attributed to mathematician, Don Coppersmith, an IBM fellow and scientist.

Say you are planning a dinner party and need to make a seating arrangement at a table, for 10 people. Some of the people don't like one another. So, you need to come up with a seating plan that all will like.

Now, if you whip out your "0-and-1 classic computer," you will find it doesn't help you at all!

Why? Because the answer to your question: "how many ways are there to arrange 10 people at a table" is: *10 factorial,* or **3,628,800...** *"three-million-six-hundred-twenty-eight-thousand eight-hundred ways."* (Phew!)

Not so easy for a classic computer! You'd need to write a fancy algorithm that identifies "who's who" and "who they each don't like." Then, your classic computer would have to run *each* of the possible seating plans until it finds *the one* that seats everyone next to someone they can tolerate. On a classic computer, it would probably run for *years!*

There are lots of real-world situations like this. Pharmaceutical companies confront mind-boggling choices in seeking vaccines and new drugs. Any choice may have this kind of situation, and it only becomes even more complex when additional factors need to be accounted for.

To address this class of problem, IBM designed the breakthrough IBM Eagle Quantum Computer in 2021. It had a 127-qubit processor that operated under the rules of quantum mechanics. Like all such quantum machines, it deals in probabilities, rather than "1s" and "0s," so it can save enormous amounts of time in seeking a correct answer by considering ALL the highest probability answers at one time, rather than one at a time! As time goes by, more problems like this will need solving and this will give us the challenges we need to perfect quantum computing.

33

THE 5G ADVANCED PHONE AND DATA NETWORK STARTS UP (2020)

THE SHEER SIZE and scope of the 5G build-out changed the plan to a terrestrial-plus-satellite network. The project is planet-wide. It involves the infrastructure of all our population, in all cities, towns, villages and countrysides. Work also aims to reach most areas of the Earth—some never before touched by telecommunication or the internet. So, the work has both a terrestrial component and a low earth orbital (LEO) satellite component. In fact, it will be the largest, most complex system that humankind has ever attempted, it must be completed—and perform perfectly if it is to be the *Big Data Network* that will integrate, coordinate and serve all our digital data devices, everywhere in the world!

The complexity of doing this is almost indescribable,

and it is far beyond the scope of this work to even try to describe it at this stage. But, look up and you will see where we will establish the workhorse of our network: a constellation of Low Earth Orbit satellites will encircle and provide data coverage of the Earth. Initially, 12,000 satellites will be *Starlink* units, placed by SpaceX.

Others will come from Blue Origin. These will make streaming news, TV, texts, instant messages, photos, stock market data, business operations, shopping carts, games, websites and movies, and cell phone calls and messaging available everywhere. But the need is beyond immense. Presently, the sheer volume of digital data trying to squeeze through our existing cellular networks is very close to exceeding their peak capacity. Every two days, it's said, present networks carry one *exabyte* of digital data. That's 1×10^{18} bytes (approximately one quintillion bytes—or, if you prefer, *one billion gigabytes!*) And our present network does not begin to cover all the Earth! So, lots more satellites and ground stations will be needed. Change will be constant for a while.

There is not very much big enough to compare to an exabyte of data. It is a lot! It has been said that five exabytes would be all the words that humans have ever spoken. Today, the average U.S. household is said to consume 190 gigabytes of data per month, and it has an average of 14.7 cell phones and internet-connected devices that include tablets, laptops, PCs, game consoles, smart TVs and appliances. As a rough measure of present "data use," consider that streaming one HD feature movie takes around 4 GB. It may sound like a lot, but experts estimate our household use of data will grow by 38 times in the next ten years. To accommodate the data speeds and volumes now foreseen to be needed, we have to go up in radio frequencies. As you go up in frequency, wavelengths get shorter and shorter until you hit *light.*

Wavelengths there are way shorter than the size of a raindrop—and they're said to be about as fragile. So power to be used up there is going to have to be higher to compensate for absorption and path losses. Count on needing a new cell phone.

Response speed and (low) latency of the network are also of prime importance. How quickly data can get from the source to a user is critical. Consider that in the heyday of the 4G network, the peak speed was (yawn!) 10 megabytes per second and latency ran 30 milliseconds! In a 5G network, the design peak speed is a snappy 10 to 20 gigabytes per second and one millisecond latency! What will be needed tomorrow?

It is said latency will have to be 1 microsecond. We'll see,

While frequencies and other specs are being finalized, the launching of low-Earth-orbit (LEO) satellites also needs to be completed. A great many LEO satellites will be needed for what will be the "new Internet" to provide continuous good, global signal coverage of all places on Earth. SpaceX and Amazon are involved in this, but information is scarce, for security reasons. The aim is to provide a new, faster, low-latency internet. The original (but slower) internet will remain in service, with its 740,000 miles of undersea fiber-optic cable that interconnects the nations of the world.)

SpaceX

SpaceX has Starlink, its constellation of LEO satellites, designed to orbit at relatively low (300–600 miles) altitudes above the Earth and to beam fast network coverage to the surface below. SpaceX initially secured licensing from the FCC to launch 12,000 satellites into orbit. It also has approval from the International Telecom Union (ITU) for use of radio frequencies to communicate with 30,000 more satellites. So, SpaceX plans to launch a total of 42,000 satellites into orbit. A number have already been placed. In the fall of 2020, an unspecified number of satellites were removed and replaced by SpaceX. No reasons were immediately available.

Amazon

Project Kuiper is the initiative from Amazon and its Blue Origin to launch a constellation of LEO satellites that will provide lowlatency, high-speed broadband connectivity to unserved and underserved communities around the world. The company says, "This is a long-term project that envisions serving tens of millions of people who lack basic access to broadband internet. We look forward to partnering on this initiative with companies that share this common vision." The Amazon constellation will use three LEO layers of satellites: 784 of them in a 590-kilometer-high orbit, 1,156 of them in a 630-kilometer orbit, and 1,296 of them in a 610 kilometer orbit. Don't be surprised if Amazon becomes your new video provider. Satellites and streaming technologies will eventually overcome old cable systems.

34

(1936 to Now) The Rise of Artificial Intelligence (AI)

The long climb of Artificial Intelligence begins back in the Vacuum Tube electronics era of 1936, in Great Britain. The driving genius of AI was then provided by Alan M. Turing. He was an early computer scientist who became fascinated by the concept that computing machines could one day be taught to "learn" and exhibit human-like intelligence and reasoning. Turing also had interests in physics, biology, neurology and chemistry, so he had ready access to knowledge that could expand on his ideas. With the electronic tools of the time, he still was able to block-out the idea of the Universal Turing Machine, the basis for the *first* computer. All digital computers today descend from Turing's concept.

Turing thought that systems could be endowed with the ability to perform tasks commonly driven by intellectual processes in human beings, including the ability to reason, to find meaning, to expand and generalize, and to learn from previous experience. So it was, that in the mid-1930s, he conceptualized an idea for a theoretical computing machine, with an unlimited memory and a "scanner" able to move back-and-forth through that memory, reading what it would find and writing it into the memory. The activities of the scanner would be controlled by a *program* also stored in the memory. But, that program could be self-updated by the computer. So, it could make its own plans! This would be *artificial general intelligence (AGI).*

This conception was dubbed *"The Universal Turing Machine."* We are still making our way toward it and AGI, but the advances over the past nearly 90 years show that we are getting there. Today, we have coined the term *Machine Learning* to describe this area of artificial intelligence.

Before moving along, make a note to yourself to discover Turing's service to England in WWII, in conquering the Nazi's *Enigma* code machine. It was another proof of his genius, courage and leadership.

After the war ended, Turing resumed his AI passion. He delivered a public lecture in London, in 1947, in which he clearly expressed what he wanted in computer intelligence. He said, "What we want is a machine that can learn from experience, and that the possibility of letting the machine alter its own instructions provides the mechanism for this." It is remarkable that Turing said this in 1947...the year when *the transistor* was invented...for, when he said it, digital computers had no such prospects. They used tubes, had little memory and occupied whole rooms. Time would have to pass, but AI and transistors grew up together. They came together with the arrival of classic, stored-natural language program, solid-state digital computers.

By 1950, Turing had devised what is now known as the "Turing Test," to reveal whether computers can "think." The test uses three participants: a human "interrogator;" a computer-and its human operator; and a human "foil." The interrogator's task is to ask questions of the other two people. Everything is done through the keyboards. One of them is on the computer. The one who is at the computer is allowed to misdirect and lie, to create false identifications. The foil must help the interrogator to make a correct identification. Multiple teams of people can play. After a time, if a significant number of players can't tell the computer from the human, the computer is considered a thinking, intelligent entity. (No AI program has passed the full Turing Test, as yet, though some are said to have come close.)

The first, true AI program was written in 1951 by Christopher Strachey at U. of Oxford in the UK. It ran on the Ferranti Mk. 1 computer at the U. of Manchester in 1952.

Also in 1952, an early AI "Machine Learning" program, called *Shopper,* was created by Anthony Oettinger at the University of Cambridge in the UK and ran on the EDSAC computer. It simulated a shopping mall of eight shops and the program could be instructed to search them for an item until it was found. While "shopping," it could remember some of the items in each shop it visited. If then sent to a shop for a remembered item, the program would instantly go directly to the shop where it had been "seen."

The next step in AI ("Machine Learning") also came along in 1952-1955, in the USA. Arthur Samuel had re-written the "checkers" program created by Christopher Stracchey for the first IBM 701 digital computer. He greatly extended its capabilities, adding the ability to "learn from experience." This was a noteworthy first effort at evolutionary computing. It pitted a modified version of a program, against the original. The winner would then become *the new standard.*

It took about 45 years for IBM to then develop *Deep Blue,* a 256-processor, stored-program, classic digital computer. In 1997, its designers challenged the World's reigning Chess Champion, Russian Garry Kasparov to play Chess...and *Deep Blue* defeated him! The computer could examine 200-million possible moves persecond, and seeahead up to 14 turns of play.

35

AI at Nvidia Today

Anyone who has followed the rise of Nvidia knows that this developer of the "GPU" (graphics processing unit) achieved a legendary position in gaming and multimedia markets by providing graphics processing units capable of delivering enhanced 3D graphics on personal computers. Founded in 1993 by Jensen Huang, Chris Malachowsky, and Curtis Priem, Nvidia focused on offloading the graphics processing task from the CPU. This inspired development of CUDA, a parallel computing platform and programming model that allowed developers to use Nvidia GPUs for general-purpose processing. This proved so effective that Nvidia GPUs went to work powering AlexNet, a deep neural network, invented by Nvidia in 2012 that won the ImageNet competition that immediately marked *the beginning of modern AI!* Through 2023, Nvidia had a meteoric rise in AI and in 2024 it became the seventh

U.S. company that is now valued at $1 trillion. The company remains a standalone tech firm, for now, and is the source of much new heat and light in modern AI. Recently, it announced it will expand its manufacturing at new plants and facilities.

Production of Blackwell chips has already begun in Phoenix, while supercomputer manufacturing plants are being developed, with mass production expected to ramp up within 12 to 15 months. NVIDIA aims to produce up to $500 billion worth of AI infrastructure over the next four years.

36

What is the Present Definition of AI?

Artificial Intelligence is now defined as the capability of a digital computer (or a robotic device) to accomplish tasks heretofore associated only with intelligent human beings. The term is most-often applied to the results of developing systems endowed with human-like intellectual functions, including the abilities to reason, to discover meaning, to generalize, or to recall and learn from past- experiences.

37

The Future of AI and Lessons of DeepSeek

The future of AI is a topic of great interest and much speculation, with many experts believing it will continue to have a profound impact on varied aspects of our lives. Here are some key trends and predictions expressed for the future of AI.

You can count on increased integration of AI into more and more industries. It will disrupt as many as it impacts: the economics of production, changing costs, timeframes and methods of production. Competitive advantages and disadvantages will also emerge, altering which of the businesses survive and prosper and which fail.

There will be major impacts through Generative AI. This refers to artificial intelligence models that create new content, such as text, images, music, or code, based on patterns learned from vast amounts of data. These models can generate realistic and creative outputs, making them useful for tasks like writing, design, and problem-solving.

AI can create lower-cost content, as well as non-time-dependent productions of materials like text, images, voice, music, teaching, speeches or other human forms of audio or video. It is likely to become greatly advanced, in time, and very widely used. It will be quite difficult to compete against generative AI, so higher-cost means will be driven-out. Already, humans, actors, entertainers and celebrities have begun "selling their avatars"... that is, the future use of their digitized, computer-animated human images and voices...to production companies, for use in future videos and entertainment programs. Animated by AI, these avatars can "stand-in" for their humans (!) and perform just as well as the original actor-person might have. This will likely lead to entirely new forms of entertainment, teaching and politics, in which the human "actors" (might be away, on tour, in the hospital, or even dead). All you then need is AI and the avatar(s) for a full, digital performance. The humans need not be available. Imagine being lectured by an Einstein-looking AI-avatar. Or, taking classes from AI avatars of the very best teachers in every subject. Think on this for awhile and see what power AI is placing within our reach. And, oh yes, once we have an AI-avatar's content, remember we have it *forever*.

Improvements in business automation will come as firms adopt AI to automate business processes previously requiring humans as operators. Operational efficiency, throughput and time-savings in decision-making are just some of the potential benefits. Decreased human headcounts will also benefit business operational and decision-making costs.

With the growth of AI, the initial challenges to be addressed will include job displacement, privacy concerns, and the ethical use of AI. While AI holds great promise, it presents complex challenges that our society needs to navigate carefully. Our goal should be to harness the benefits of AI while mitigating potential risks and ensuring that ongoing AI developments align with human values and needs. We also need vigilant, strong law enforcement to deal with evil users.

AI technologies will surely evolve rapidly, with ongoing research and development in areas such as machine learning, deep learning, and neural networks. In time, AI will become ingrained in our daily lives, influencing everything from how personal assistants work, to use of our cars, robot taxis and smart home devices. The benefit will prove to be making our interactions with technology much more natural and intuitive. But, as AI comes into wider and wider use, real emphasis needs to be given to making it very, very secure, trustworthy and sustainable.

If AI can be easily "hacked," it will pose real and serious dangers, because it can be used to generate "false personas" that other people (say, banks and credit card firms) might accept as "you." In the hands of a criminal, hacked AI could be a very serious problem to recover from.

The initial challenges of AI have included job displacement, privacy concerns, and safe, ethical use. While AI holds great promise, it presents a complex challenge that our society needs to plan and navigate very carefully. Our aim must be to harness the benefits of AI while mitigating potential risks and ensuring that ongoing AI developments align with human values and needs. We also need vigilant, strong laws and enforcement, to deal with evil AI users. AI that has been too-quickly adopted has failed in a number of companies.

AI technologies will surely evolve, with ongoing research and development in areas such as machine learning, deep learning, and neural networks. In time, AI will become ingrained in our daily lives, influencing everything from how personal assistants work, to use of our cars, robot taxis, robotic and other smart home devices. The benefit will prove to be making our interactions with technology much more natural and intuitive. But, as AI comes into wider and wider use, real emphasis needs to be given to making it very, very secure, trustworthy and sustainable. If AI can be easily "hacked," it will pose real and serious dangers, because it can be used to generate "false personas" that other people (say, banks and credit card firms) might accept as "you." In the hands of a criminal, hacked AI could be a very serious problem to recover from.

AI presents a very complex challenge that society must navigate very carefully. The goal will be to harness the benefits of AI, while reducing the other potential risks to users by ensuring that AI-based solutions are made truly ethical, sustainable and very secure.

The Chinese DeepSeek Incident offers serious lessons to us about the panic that can result when ignorance meets AI. If you missed it, in late January, 2025, U.S. news reports from China reported that a Chinese start-up company named DeepSeek had achieved artificial intelligence comparable to or exceeding the performance of Chat-GPT and other top American AI Models. The Chinese Model was said to have been engineered by "young geniuses," using older Nvidia chips that had not been blocked by U.S. export restrictions. The release also disclosed that, unlike AI Models of the U.S. firms, all of which were "closed" (not explained or not available for study to outsiders), the DeepSeek Model was "open" and it could be freely downloaded online. And so, its architecture and software were free to all! Also, the cost of producing the Deepsake Model and training it was said to be only about 10% ($6 million) of the costs spent to produce and train Chat-GPT and other U.S. AI Models.

The DeepSeek news hit the U.S. stock market like a bombshell! It triggered panic, massive stock selling. In one day, Nvidia lost *600-billion dollars in market* *capitalization*, as market participants panicked and sold in an incredible stampede, fearing that "China was ahead of the U.S. in the war for AI leadership." This news instantly raised serious panic and economic concerns about future U.S. dominance in AI.

Impact on U.S. Companies Stocks: The announcement caused a sharp decline in the stock prices of major U.S. tech companies, especially those involved in AI and chip manufacturing. Nvidia, a key player in AI technology, saw its stock price drop by 17%, wiping out nearly $600 billion in market value of its stock.

Overall Market Reaction: The Nasdaq Composite, which is heavily influenced by tech stocks, fell by 3.1%, while the S&P 500 dropped by 1.5%. Traders were worried about the potential impact of cheaper AI technology on the profitability and market share of U.S. companies.

Implications: The sell-off highlighted growing competition in the AI sector and raised questions about the sustainability of current valuations for AI-related stocks. It also underscored the growing geopolitical and economic competition between the U.S. and China in the field of AI.

Insight: Fear of such unknowns, among people with no electronics or AI knowledge to oppose it, played a significant role in market behavior. When traders encountered unexpected developments, in things they'd never been educated in, it led to uncertainty, then, panic-selling, because they lacked the immediate knowledge to fully assess the true implications of the new situation. Few understand AI and could not realize that Deepseek's "training" might have been "pilfered." (So, of course it would be *cheap!)* Word later came that the Chinese had hacked the computer AI-training files of ChatGPT and trained their AI with our files (which cost us many million $ to create.)

The cumulative result was the largest one-day loss in market capitalization ever sustained by the U.S. stock market! In their ignorance, traders didn't know, so they "thought the Chinese were ahead of us" and over-reacted. It was a situation parallel to the "Sputnik panic" of the 1950s, when the Soviet Union launched a basketball-sized satellite that sent out radio "beeps" as it circled the Earth. The huge uproar from then-space-ignorant America was that "the Russians are ahead of us," and that panic got America into the "space race." We did quite well, of course. And all that Sputnik ever did was *beep*.

Results: The initial trigger was the DeepSeek announcement itself. But, the resulting trading panic and sell-off were magnified by IGNORANCE, triggering a general lack of understanding (because market participants had never been educated in school about electronics or AI). So they had fears of the implications, and that triggered panicked behavior, to avoid the unknown. The combination created a feedback loop, where selling caused more selling, as stockholders rushed to avoid unknown risk that appeared to be growing larger every minute.

Cooler Heads Find Several Great Results: As the ashes of the selloff were examined by AI experts, their findings pointed to the beneficial results of China having gone public and open-source with DeepSeek. First, it showed that AI can be achieved using a wide range of chips. Those who have downloaded the Model have tried it in all manner of digital devices, down to the "Raspberry Pi" units that sell for as little as $35. Performance is way-less on these, but—hey! It works.

Second is the proof that new economy is made possible in training, by having a "smart," established Model train a new Model, just coming on-line. (If you ask DeepSeek V3 "who are you," it will answer "Chat-GPT" (that's the designation of its American training model. Through this, we've learned that AI can get lots cheaper after the initial Model is trained. It then becomes the "teacher" of the next AI Model we make, with as much as 90% savings! (This became known because the Chinese hacked and stole Chat-GPT's training files, and Deepseek ratted-them-out when it answered "Chat-GPT" to the question: "who are you?")

Third is discovery of the phenomenon of "growth in smartness." In second and subsequent generations of Models, when a "Teacher AI" trains a "Student AI" it imparts *extra data* that makes the Student AI "smarter." Finally. One can only hope that this Deepseek incident on the part of China will lead to improved, co-operation between East and West in years to come, and that enlightened interest will also be shown by all those charged with education of our children in the U.S. not to overlook the teaching of American electronics (and AI), history, civics, handwriting and other foolishly deleted subjects. It would be very unwise to send America's Golden Era children into the 21st century future, supported only by a 19th century education!

38

A Review of Google, Amazon Web Services, NVIDIA and Microsoft

IN THE EVER-EVOLVING digital electronics / AI landscape, four high technology giants stand out for their transformative contributions: *Google, Amazon Web Services (AWS), NVIDIA and Microsoft*. Each of these companies has carved a unique niche, impacting various aspects of electronic/AI technology, from search engines and cloud computing to software development and artificial intelligence. This review delves into the strengths, innovations, and market positions of these tech titans, providing a comprehensive overview of their roles in shaping our future.

Google

Overview

Founded in 1998 by Larry Page and Sergey Brin, Google began as a search engine and has since expanded its horizons to encompass a plethora of services and products. Today, Google is a subsidiary of Alphabet Inc., its parent company, and is synonymous with innovation and technological prowess.

Key Products and Services

- Search Engine: Google's search engine is the most widely used in the world, processing over 3.5 billion searches per day. It employs sophisticated algorithms and machine learning to deliver accurate and relevant results.
- Google Cloud: Google Cloud offers a suite of cloud computing services, including data storage, machine learning, and analytics. It competes directly with AWS and Microsoft Azure.
- Android: Google's mobile operating system, Android, powers a majority of the world's smartphones, providing a platform for millions of apps and developers.

- Gmail: With over 1.5 billion active users, Gmail is one of the most popular email services globally, known for its user- friendly interface and robust security features.
- YouTube: Acquired by Google in 2006, YouTube is the leading video-sharing platform, with billions of monthly active users and a vast library of content.

Innovations

Google is at the forefront of technological innovation, particularly in artificial intelligence (A.I.) and machine learning. Projects like Google DeepMind and the development of AI-powered assistants such as Google Assistant showcase the company's commitment to pushing the boundaries of what's possible.

Market Position

Google's dominance in the search engine market is unparalleled, holding a present market share of over 90%. Its advertising platform, Google Ads, is a significant revenue driver, contributing to the company's robust financial performance. Google Cloud, while trailing AWS and Azure, is a formidable player in the cloud computing space, continuously expanding its market share.

Amazon Web Services (AWS)

Overview

Launched in 2006, Amazon Web Services (AWS) is the cloud computing arm of Amazon, the e-commerce giant founded by Jeff Bezos. AWS has revolutionized the way businesses operate by providing scalable and cost-effective cloud solutions.

Key Products and Services

- Compute Services: AWS offers a range of compute services, including EC2 (Elastic Compute Cloud) for scalable virtual servers and Lambda for serverless computing.
- Storage Services: Amazon S3 (Simple Storage Service) and Amazon Glacier provide robust and scalable storage solutions for enterprises.
- Database Services: AWS offers a variety of database services, including Amazon RDS (Relational Database Service) and Amazon DynamoDB for NoSQL databases.
- Machine Learning: AWS provides machine learning services such as Amazon SageMaker, which enables developers to build, train, and deploy machine learning models at scale.

- Networking: AWS's networking services, including Amazon VPC (Virtual Private Cloud) and AWS Direct Connect, allow businesses to create secure and high-performance networks.

Innovations

AWS has been a pioneer in cloud computing, constantly introducing new services and features to meet the evolving needs of businesses. Its innovations in serverless computing, machine learning, and edge computing have set industry standards and paved the way for future advancements.

Market Position

AWS is the undisputed leader in the cloud computing market, holding a significant market share. Its customer base spans startups, enterprises, and government agencies, all of whom rely on AWS's reliable and scalable infrastructure. The company's continuous growth and innovation have solidified its position as the go-to cloud provider.

Amazon's recent entry into the IC chip-making space, particularly in the AI segment, is a significant move. The company has been developing its own AI chips, such as the Graviton processors, *Inferentia*, and *Trainium* series, to enhance its cloud services and reduce reliance on third-party suppliers, like AMD and Intel.

The Trainium3 is particularly noteworthy. Built with TSMC's 3-nanometer technology, it promises to be twice as fast and 40% more energy-efficient than its predecessor, Trainium2. This positions Amazon to compete more effectively with NVIDIA, which currently dominates the AI chip market.

Amazon's strategy to develop and manufacture its own chips allows for greater control over its technology infrastructure, leading to potential cost savings and innovation in AI services. This move also aligns with the broader trend of Big Tech companies like Microsoft and Meta entering the semiconductor space to hedge against supply chain issues and reduce dependence on external AI chip suppliers.

Overall, Amazon's initiative in IC chip-making in the AI segment is a bold and strategic move that could reshape the competitive landscape in the industry.

Microsoft

Overview

Founded in 1975 by Bill Gates and Paul Allen, Microsoft has evolved from a software company into a global technology leader. With its diverse portfolio of products and services, Microsoft continues to influence various sectors, from enterprise software to gaming.

Key Products and Services

- Microsoft Windows: The flagship operating system, Windows, is used by billions of devices worldwide, making it a cornerstone of Microsoft's success.
- Microsoft Office: The Office suite, including Word, Excel, and PowerPoint, remains the industry standard for productivity software.
- Microsoft Azure: Azure is Microsoft's cloud computing platform, offering a wide range of services, including virtual machines, databases, and AI tools.
- LinkedIn: Acquired by Microsoft in 2016, LinkedIn is the world's largest professional networking platform, with over 700 million users.
- Xbox: Microsoft's gaming console, Xbox, has a loyal following and a rich library of games, contributing to the company's entertainment segment.

Innovations

Microsoft's innovation extends across various domains, from cloud computing and AI to quantum computing and mixed reality. Projects like HoloLens, an augmented reality headset, and Azure Quantum, a quantum computing platform, exemplify Microsoft's forward-thinking approach.

Microsoft's Morgana chip, also known as Majorana 1, is powered by a ground-breaking semiconductor-superconductor hybrid material called a *topoconductor*. This innovative material enables the creation of topological superconductivity, a new state of matter, which is harnessed to produce more stable and scalable qubits. These advancements are paving the way for transformative quantum computing solutions. This material combines indium arsenide (a semiconductor) and aluminum (a superconductor) to create a new state of matter known as *topological superconductivity*. This enables the formation of *Majorana Zero Modes*, which are building blocks of Microsoft's topological qubits. These qubits are more stable, scalable, and efficient compared to traditional ones, paving the way for quantum computers capable of solving very complex industrial and societal challenges.

The Majorana 1 chip is designed to scale up to a million qubits on a single chip, a milestone that could revolutionize fields like health-care, AI, and materials science. It's an exciting glimpse into the future of computing!

Market Position

Microsoft is a dominant player in both the software and cloud computing markets. Azure, its cloud platform, is a strong competitor to AWS, with a rapidly growing market share. Microsoft's enterprise solutions, like Office 365 and Dynamics 365, are widely adopted by businesses across the globe. The company's financial stability and continuous innovation make it a powerhouse in the tech industry. Microsoft is also a contender in quantum computing, through its discoveries in *topo-conductors*. As this discovery matures, quantum computing will gain in the number of noise-resistant qubits it can field in new quantum computers, and these will be able to reliably handle increasingly complex tasks, eventually making the classic 0and-1 digital computer into a quaint, obsolete relic.

NVIDIA

Company Overview

NVIDIA is an American multinational technology company specializing in graphics processing units (GPUs), artificial intelligence (AI), and accelerated computing. Founded in 1993 by Jensen Huang, Chris Malachowsky, and Curtis Priem, the company is headquartered in Santa Clara, California. Core Business & Products

NVIDIA is a leader in GPU technology, powering industries such as gaming, AI, data centers, automotive, and healthcare. Its GeForce GPUs dominate the gaming market, while NVIDIA RTX revolutionizes graphics with AI-powered ray tracing. The company also develops AI chips, cloud computing solutions, and autonomous vehicle technology.

Financial Performance
As of FY 2025, NVIDIA reported $130.57 billion in revenue, with $72.88 billion in net income. The company continues to expand its market presence, with a $1 trillion available market opportunity.

Innovation & AI Leadership
NVIDIA pioneered accelerated computing, enabling breakthroughs in deep learning, AI factories, and digital twins. Its *CUDA* platform supports AI development, and *Omniverse* facilitates industrial digitalization. The company powers AI-driven healthcare, robotics, and autonomous vehicles.

Global Impact & Recognition
NVIDIA was recognized as one of America's Best Companies (2025) by Forbes, and among the World's Most Innovative Companies. With 36,000+ employees across 38 countries, it continues to shape the future of computing.

Market Position
1. AI Chips & Accelerators
NVIDIA controls 70% to 95% of the AI GPU market, making its H100 and H200 chips essential for AI model training and inference. Despite rising competition, its *CUDA* platform remains a major advantage.

2. AI Data Centers & Cloud Computing
Other tech giants are committing billions to AI infrastructure, ensuring ongoing, continued demand for NVIDIA's GPUs in data centers and cloud AI services to come.

AI Agents & Enterprise Software
NVIDIA is expanding into AI agent software, targeting a $1 trillion market. Its *NeMo* microservices allow businesses to build autonomous AI systems, enhancing enterprise AI adoption.

Robotics & Autonomous Systems
NVIDIA sees robotics as its next big AI opportunity, integrating AI into self-driving cars, humanoid robots, and industrial automation.

Sovereign AI & National AI Programs
Governments worldwide are investing in sovereign AI, creating nation-specific AI models. NVIDIA is well-positioned to supply the necessary infrastructure.

In Conclusion:
Google, Amazon Web Services, Microsoft and NVIDIA are four pillars of the modern, 21st century technology landscape. Each company has quite unique strengths and contributions, driving progress in their respective domains.

Google's search engine, Amazon AWS's cloud computing services, Microsoft's software and topological conductor solutions, and NVIDIA's generative AI and robotic achievements will go on collectively transforming the way we live, work, and interact with technology. As these tech titans continue to innovate and expand, their influence on the electronics/AI digital world will undoubtedly grow, reshaping the future in ways we can now only begin to imagine. Also, at any time, the market may be disrupted by any of the many smaller AI firms, through innovation and acquisition by a deep-pocketed firm (like IBM). Time will tell.

39

THE U.S. GOLDEN ERA: THE START OF A NEW BEGINNING

As THESE WORDS are written, the United States of America is embarked on "re-industrializing." Translation: regaining the power of manufacturing things here in the U.S. It's estimated that globalization, past (bad) government trade policies, corruption, bureaucracy, theft, restrictive laws, and corporate greed for higher profits, all resulted in the incredible, cumulative loss, over decades, of 97, 000 manufacturing businesses...factories that were shipped to other countries, taking millions of our good U.S. jobs with them!

The turnaround championed by U.S. President Donald J. Trump's administration is to "Make America Great Again." He made huge promises (which he has kept) in his presidential campaign, 80-million American voters responded by electing him, plus a majority of

Republicans in Congress. His public approval is an all-time-high for U.S. presidents. Despite the erroneous negative predictions by most economists (who clearly were wrong) he proposed *tariffs* on countries who had all profited greatly at our expense by not trading fairly, and/or by looting us of many businesses and jobs. (A tariff is an "admission tax" paid to the American government on goods foreign countries want to sell within the U.S. Many of them have long had higher tariffs and trading restrictions that have prevented or hindered U.S. firms from selling in *their* countries for as long as the past 60 years! This cheating has now been stopped. If a manufacturer from a foreign country wants to avoid U.S. tariffs, they can pay zero tariff in two ways: either by manufacturing their products here in the U.S., employing our citizens; or, by dropping their tariff charges on U.S. goods sold in their country to zero. We will do the same, so trade will truly be fair. This major trade policy change is driving the re-industrialization of the U.S. as manufacturers relocate here to enjoy lower costs and very beneficial treatment.

The electronics and AI segment, and businesses that derive from their use will especially find a welcoming environment here, *in the place where electronics began!* Opportunities abound! New, great incentives to the world to manufacture in the U. S. are being given to attract the cream of scientific, technical and global manufacturing firms, individuals, as well as investments by wealthy countries to establish businesses here, and hire in the U.S. Those who want to manufacture "there," but "sell in the U.S." must pay tariffs to gain that privilege. This reverses the long-followed, old (and quite brainlessly liberal) U.S. practice of our paying tariffs to sell in other countries, but not charging them any tariff to sell here! TheTrump policy seeks to repatriate and restore our onshore manufacturing capabilities, substantially increase U.S. employment opportunities. and vastly increase our national, state, family and personal incomes, also seeking to eliminate personal income taxes on individuals and families, so that America's people can keep more of what their work earns. The Trump policy also encourages legal U.S. migration by top business owners and wealthy investors who will establish new businesses here in the U.S., as well as encouraging legal emigration by highly ranked technical, scientific and other gifted individuals who will become educated about America, enjoy the fruits of living and working here, and learn to love the U.S. for all the freedoms that it stands for. The nation will need a great many more high-merit, good people, to staff all the many opportunities that take root here.

It promises to be America's Golden Era, and it is open to everyone willing to help make it happen. Think it over. Consider your tomorrow. Invest your time wisely. Now that you've read this book and know how electronics and AI got us to the front door of The Golden Era, think about where you'd like to be tomorrow. If you now hear music, perhaps the sweet song being played is "God Bless America."

***

Dear Reader: Here's to Your Future!

I hope that you have enjoyed this book and that it has done the job I intended—namely, to share with you the origins, inventors and history that have propelled us across centuries, from the beginning of *American electronics, to the AI technology of today*. I've tried to tell you lots of things nobody's ever told you before about how we got to where we are in electronics and A.I., on our way to a brighter tomorrow. I hope this has encouraged you to learn more about electronics and AI ...and to use all the wonderful resources we now have in our libraries, books and online sources to advance your knowledge. You've begun...now, use what you've learned to go further!

Because the right (and very best) woman in the whole world married me in 1966, I have been encouraged to keep on finding and writing stories about people like you (and me) who've had some wonderful ideas (like Chapter 1's Mr. Conforti, of piano fame) who took us very far in what we now love in music. I thank God for her, and for you! I have tried to faithfully tell the stories of our innovators to the best of my ability. It's taken a lifetime to find them. It is my fervent hope that you will have a better sense of the future you will live in by knowing the wonderful accomplishments of the good folks who helped to make it happen. Please honor them.

Perhaps you'll also go on to be one of them?

***

Please do leave a review. Your opinion matters most to folks who, just like you, are trying to decide if this is "the book" to choose. Please help them to choose this one. You'll be doing everyone (and me) a favor! Thanks and 73. (*"best regards"*) and do go far in Electronics & AI!

George J. Whalen, NY9A

About the Author

George J. Whalen is an electronics engineer, marketer, inventor, lifelong amateur radio hobbyist (NY9A), and prolific nonfiction writer in technology and electronics. He holds a number of patents, has published a great many electronics and tech articles, print books and (soon) one audiobook. Print books include Electronics in 2 Hours, Artificial Intelligence in 3; The Story of Radio to 5G Wireless; Automotive Electronics; Solid State Ignition; Home Wiring; Popular Science – How It Works: Illustrated, and many more. He graduated as an adult with a B.S. (distinction) in 1984 from Iona, in New Rochelle, NY. He specialized in electronic technology marketing and became a senior executive at a well-known Fortune 100 tech firm for 15 years, before incorporating and opening his own tech marketing consultancy for another 15. He's served a great many U.S. and international electronic publishing, printing equipment and industrial technology clients and is an avid student of technology history, A.I., inventors, electronics and radio, their little-known stories, and how their technologies evolve over time. Now the self-publisher of this, all-new: Electronics in 2 Hours, Artificial Intelligence in 3, as well as the new edition of his first book (from 1970): How The Electrical System Works In Your '70s Classic U.S. Car, an auto electrical system sourcebook on classic '60s through '80s U.S. cars for folks who lovingly restore these incomparable vehicles. Others of his published books cover technology, science, and electronics projects.

List of Sources. The author gratefully acknowledges the assistance contributed by the following.

Archives and Libraries of Yale U. and Harvard U., Google;

Archives and Library of Columbia U., Armstrong Memorial Research Foundation; Jennfer Comins, Archivist; Bell Labs, Nokia. Congress of the United States: Dagogo Alltraide, Author and Producer; Edward A. Sharpe, Archivist, SW Museum of Engrng, Glendale, AZ; Electronics Notes.com, Ian Poole, Ed; Federal Communications Commission; Ford Motor Company. General Motors Corporation.

Chrysler Corporation; Wikipedia.org (Special thanks to Wikipedia Editors for their much-admired content); Institute of Electrical and Electronics Engineers (IEEE); Intel; SAE International; SpaceX; Statista; Skyworks; Rhode & Schwarz; Virgin.

IBM Corp. (Much admired for its legendary contributions to electronics and AI; watch for new quantum computing advances by 2029).

The Saga of the Vacuum Tube, Gerald F. J. Tyne, BSEE (ex-8KN); author of 23 great articles in Radio news.

Man of High Fidelity: Edwin Howard Armstrong; Lawrence Lessing, Bantam Books, March 1969; a superb biography.

Dr. Joshua Levy, PhD and Historian, The Library of Congress, Washington, DC; a very special friend.

Special thanks to another dear friend: Patti McEvoy: One of my former editors at Popular Electronics.

Larry Steckler, my friend and former editor and publisher at Radio-Electronics Magazine.

Cover Design and Treatment: Our wonderful son: Russell Whalen, at Printability.com

Grandson: Cameron Whalen. Who will live in the next century and know how it all turns out!

APPENDIX 1

HISTORIC PATENTS BY INVENTORS DESCRIBED EARLIER IN THIS BOOK

U.S. patent copies can be obtained free from Google Patents (at www.google.com patent search). Some are made from paper documents of very great age. Time impacts them, and they may be hard to read, but these older patents present the genius of yesterday and will give you insight into the ways great minds of yesterday turned ideas about into reality.

US129971 Mahlon G. Loomis Discoverer of Radio
US307031 Thomas A. Edison; Edison Effect
US803684 J Ambrose Fleming; First Electronics VT Diode
US2524035 John Bardeen, Walter Brattain & William Shockley Point Contact Transistor

US2904662 Dawon Kahng & Mohammed Atalla; (Bell Labs) MOSFET Transistor

US1050441 Reginald A. Fessenden; AM Radio Broadcasting

US1773980 Philo T. Farnsworth; All-Electronic TV System

US2292387 Hedy (Kiesler) Lamarr (Markey) & George Antheil; Auto Switching/CDMA

US5121407 Jesse E. Russell; Digital Network & Cellphone System

US4136359 Steven G. Wozniak; Apple; Best personal computer ever!

US3115581A Jack S. Barkus; Integrated Circuit (Nobel Prize)

US2981877 Robert Noyce; Integrated Circuit

APPENDIX 2

More About "The Electric Start" of 1844–1912

Decades before "Electronics" actually came, we had "The Electric Start," where geniuses like Morse, Loomis, Bell, Hertz and Tesla created huge leaps forward, without using tubes or transistors. I set the beginning of American Electronics at the 1868 U.S. mountaintop experiment of Mahlon Loomis, followed by the monumental work of James Clerk Maxwell (a genius Scot physicist and dean) who theorized and established a mathematical proof of the existence of electromagnetic (EM) waves (think radio-to-light waves) in his foundational and magnificent 1873 treatise. These waves had been proven to exist in 1886 by German physicist-genius Heinrich Hertz using electric sparks (which create very unruly EM waves). His spark lab apparatus was copied by Marconi and others, to create ship-to-shore spark wireless telegraphy. (By the way: Guglielmo Marconi started out as a wonderful amateur radio hobbyist and inventor. He had the funds to pioneer spark wireless though he had not the foggiest idea how radio worked and said so when receiving the 1909 Nobel Prize in Physics!) Guglielmo Marconi was born into a family with both aristocratic and entrepreneurial roots. His father, Giuseppe Marconi, was an Italian aristocratic landowner from Porretta Terme, while his mother, Annie Jameson, was Irish and the granddaughter of John Jameson, the founder of famous *Jameson Irish whiskey.)* Marconi himself was ennobled as a marquess in 1929, by King Victor Emmanuel III of Italy. His family, while not royalty, was definitely part of the aristocracy. Marconi himself went on to achieve great wealth through his pioneering work in wireless communication.

Mahlon Loomis' experiment of 1868 created "square waves" of switched DC power through one 600-foot-long copper wire kite antenna (and ground), radiated as an EM wave to an identical-length kite antenna (and ground) at a receive-location 18 miles away. Both were on mountain-tops in Virginia. The identical antennas would be self-resonant at about the same frequency. Since a square wave contains harmonics of all frequencies, the self-resonance of the duplicate 600' wire antennas would cause both to "ring" at one specific frequency, causing a burst EM wave to be sent-and-received at some low frequency. This was radio.

This same period brought Edison's 1880 electric light bulbs (and their perplexing black spots), and the "Edison effect" around 1895; then, the invention of the diode vacuum tube in 1897, by John Ambrose Fleming). Meanwhile, naturalized American genius, Nikola Tesla had arrived in the U.S. from Serbia in 1890 and he had already made extraordinary contributions to science and engineering by then. His work revolved around electrical power systems, induction motors and machinery powered by AC. He refined designs for AC generators, transformers, and motors, laying the groundwork for modern electrical grids. His "Tesla coils" found use in spark transmitters and other items he patented were radio essentials. His groundbreaking theories established him as a visionary and he contributed much to the future of electronics. (A lifelong futurist, his predictions of autonomous vehicles, remote control systems like today's "drones," and pocket-size units for global personal wireless, as well as x-ray imaging and radar systems all were uncannily early).

Don't miss out!

Visit the website below and you can sign up to receive emails whenever George J. Whalen NY9A publishes a new book. There's no charge and no obligation.

www.https://books2read.com/r/B-A-UXAX-GFTBG

BOOKS 2 READ

Connecting independent readers to independent writers.

www.ingramcontent.com/pod-product-compliance
Lightning Source LLC
LaVergne TN
LVHW052327200926
848481LV00002B/688